Midlife Happy Hour

Midlife Happy Hour

Our Reward for Surviving Careers, Kids, and Chaos

Elaine Ambrose

Midlife Happy Hour:
Our Reward for Surviving Careers, Kids, and Chaos

Brown Books Publishing Group
16250 Knoll Trail Drive, Suite 205
Dallas, Texas 75248
www.BrownBooks.com
(972) 381-0009

A New Era in Publishing®

ISBN 9781612549217
LCCN 2016938261

Printed in the United States
10 9 8 7 6 5 4 3 2 1

Book cover and design by Sarah Tregay, DesignWorks Creative, Inc.
Author photo by Dorothy Salvatori

For more information or to contact the author, please go to www.ElaineAmbrose.com

This book is dedicated to my spirited granddaughters.

They already know that laughter is the best medicine.

Books by Elaine Ambrose

Midlife Cabernet

Drinking with Dead Women Writers – with AK Turner

Drinking with Dead Drunks – with AK Turner

Menopause Sucks – with Joanne Kimes

The Red Tease – A Woman's Adventures in Golf

Gators & Taters – A Week of Bedtime Stories

The Magic Potato – La Papa Mágica

Waiting for the Harvest

Elaine's Short Stories and Poems Appear in the Following Anthologies

Faith, Hope & Healing – Dr. Bernie Siegel

A Miracle Under the Christmas Tree

The Dog with the Old Soul

Hauntings from the Snake River Plain

Tales from the Attic

Beyond Burlap

Daily Erotica – 366 Poems of Passion

Little White Dress

Feisty After 45

Contents

Author's Note

The kids are grown, the menstrual periods stopped, and we survived four decades of dealing with corporate clowns. We're ready to party.

Middle-aged women know that it's more fun to celebrate than to stab someone with a fork and deal with the messy court case and jail time. Good friends, laughter, and a bottle of wine are what every woman needs while adjusting to empty nests and full schedules, hyperactive adult children and ailing parents, and loose skin and tight budgets. We no longer believe the lie that we could do it all: Bring home the bacon, fry it in a designer pan, raise delightful children, and strut in stilettos with perky boobs bobbing to please our man. That myth contains more baloney that a cheap sandwich in a truck stop deli.

There are more than 40 million middle-aged women in the United States, and a significant number of us are ready for a break after decades of working various jobs, managing (or imagining) lovers, and solving one crisis after another. Sharing good times together allows women to enjoy the rewards for living long enough to see the kids grow up, the mortgage decrease, and the bad boss get indicted. We did our time, and now the youngsters can take over and sashay through the doors we struggled to open for them. After all we've endured, we want to laugh. Now.

My Midlife Happy Hour Club is a gregarious group of tenacious women who meet sporadically to celebrate festive occasions: birthdays, a cure for irritable bowel syndrome, a Hollywood movie with a leading actress over 40, or the fact that a sales clerk actually noticed us. We gather for Happy Hour, the best time of our lives. We aren't ready for closing time but prepared to celebrate a time of life when women finally get to sit down, raise a glass to toast the day, and boldly declare, "I'm relevant, resilient, and ready for another round."

Early Signs I Wasn't Eligible for Sainthood

I suspected at a young age that my parents didn't like me. When I was five years old, they gave me scissors and told me to go outside and run around. Mom allowed me to ride in the front seat of her car, usually standing up without restraint. My dad introduced the family by saying, "I have two outstanding children. And Elaine." My suspicions were confirmed when they dropped me off at college and sped away. I was on to them.

I was born as a total disappointment and retained that dubious distinction throughout my childhood. I survived next to my dead sister in my mother's womb and should have been hailed as one tough little fighter, but no. After I emerged all ready to be adored and cuddled, my father shook his head and left the hospital as his exhausted wife meekly apologized for the transgression of having a girl. Even as a newborn baby, I must have sensed that it wasn't cozy in my bright, new world because I wailed for an hour until some exasperated nurse shoved a bottle in my mouth. That powerful incident probably accounts for my future weight problems, and in all honesty, contributed significantly to my need as an adult to have some kind of bottle nearby.

When I was old enough to ask about my twin sister, my mother only commented that the baby had died sometime before birth. Two bassinets were waiting in the delivery room, but the first baby, named Arlene, was born dead. I could only imagine the utter dismay my father would have felt if he had wasted his time and energy on siring and supporting *two* female children. He probably would have hung black curtains over the door and lamented his misfortune over another glass of Crown Royal at the Silver Spur, the local saloon in the village of Wendell, Idaho. The grizzled men sitting around the bar would have nodded in solemn agreement through the smoke-filled room, mumbling with pity about his great calamity. In a small farming community, more sons meant more workers in the field.

"Too bad about them females," ol' Titus would mutter, a toothpick bobbing between his chapped lips as he spoke. "Can't get much work out of a girl."

"I suppose one would be tolerable," I imagined my father answering. "The wife needs help during the canning season and she's always behind with mending my socks. A girl could help with the household chores."

"Remember what happened to Burt," the bartender would mention as he wiped the sticky bar with a dirty cloth. "Had six headstrong girls and they all got themselves into trouble. I heard some of them moved to an apartment in Boise and got jobs. Can you imagine?" Heads would collectively shake in dismay and another round of shots would be ordered. Woe to the man who raised a herd of rebellious girls. Burt, an empty shell of a man, and his submissive wife eventually moved away and never returned.

A few years later, the same men at the bar cheered and passed cigars when my father proudly announced the grand and glorious birth of another son. Again, he was king of the county. The Crown Royal, the Deluxe Extra-Rare Edition, was passed around and backs were slapped in a manly manner.

Over the years, much to my father's irritation, I refused to accept my assigned status as a less desirable human. My rebellion began as a toddler when I refused to wear the dresses my mother sewed for me. Instead, I pulled on my brother's clothes and preferred playing in mud to playing with dolls. By age five, I loved running outside and on more than one occasion I threw off my shirt so I could play Cowboys and Indians with my brothers and their friends. My mother would come yelling out the door, drag me inside, and punish me for showing off my flat chest. At the time, I couldn't understand why only boys got to do fun things like remove their shirts and pee standing up.

By age ten, my hair was long and disheveled, my dress was rumpled from playing outside, and my black glasses proclaimed that I was impaired. My parents already had decided that I was a Problem Child. There had been too many calls to the school principal's office to discuss my noisy and disruptive behavior in class. Obviously, at that time, there was no appreciation for my spirited nature. Or, my teachers complained that I daydreamed too much. They didn't buy my excuse that creative children needed time for imagination and reflection. And, my parents were weary of my fights with my brothers, noting that "The boys never questioned" the rigid rules of our home.

My brothers received special treatment. They had reloading sets in their bedrooms that enabled them to fill shotgun shells with ammunition, and they were allowed to shoot rock chucks from the porch and hang their guns on the wall. They shot pheasants in the pasture and dumped the lifeless bodies in the kitchen sink for my mother to silently pluck, clean, and cook. I had a sewing kit and a record player. When chores were finished and dinner dishes washed, I escaped to my room where I played my music from The Beach Boys. "In My Room" from their 1963 album was a personal favorite. By 1964, I had secretly acquired the "Meet the Beatles" album, and I turned down the volume and played it several times while singing into my hairbrush microphone.

My next rebellious act was to shave my legs. I was twelve when my mother sat beside me, nervously cleared her throat, and gave this serious admonishment: I was never to shave my legs. I solemnly nodded but neglected to mention that I secretly had been shaving for more than a year.

My mother never had shaved her legs, mainly because respectable women of the era didn't engage in such pretentious behavior and also she didn't have any noticeable hair. On the other hand (or leg), my sudden eruption of hair rivaled a tangled clump of Spanish moss growing on two logs in a hot swamp. At age eleven, I endured a cataclysmic growth spurt of such epic proportions that my legs mutated into furry poles covered with twisted hairballs. All I saw between my plaid skirts and saddle shoes were two mangy pelts that should have been hanging from a trapper's rope. Within months, my legs were hairy enough to attract nesting rodents.

In my young angst, I noticed that hair was sprouting in other places, too. After a private examination of my changing body, I was convinced that somehow there had been a big mistake and my new carpet of pubic hair wouldn't stop where it should. I feared that soon there would be one long growth of hair that reached from my crotch to my ankles. My *World Book Encyclopedias* didn't provide any answers, except to show freaky photos of bearded women in the circus. I inspected my chin and didn't see any beard but decided I had to act.

Our small home only had one bathroom, so we all stored our toiletries in the cabinet beside the sink. That's where I saw my father's razor and made the decision to attack my fur. Looking back, I'm mortified that I resorted to such drastic measures, but there was no time to waste. Summer was coming I didn't want to resemble a monkey in shorts.

The first attempts were painful as I scraped the stubborn hair from my legs. Nicks and cuts bled onto the floor, and I quickly blotted the wounds with toilet paper. I saw a bottle of aftershave tonic so I smeared some on my battered legs. That's the first time I learned how to scream in silence. I cleaned up the mess, returned everything to the cabinet, and hobbled to bed. The next day I read the bottles more closely and decided I would use shaving cream and warm water, as soon as the scabs healed.

I perfected the routine over the next few months and was proud of my smooth, long legs. I noticed my mother was buying more razor blades, and she mentioned that my father's beard was getting so mature and healthy that the blades were wearing out faster than normal. Again, I solemnly nodded, secretly delighted that my legs no longer belonged on a buffalo.

Disaster struck in late July. I fell off my horse, broke my leg, and needed a plaster cast from my knee to my toes. I worried about what was happening beneath the cast and inspected the casing daily for tufts of fur that might emerge while I continued to shave the other leg. After two months, it was time to remove the cast. I nervously sat on the doctor's examination table with my legs stretched out in front of me. My mother focused on the cast to be sure the doctor's noisy saw wouldn't accidentally cut off my leg. Finally, the plaster broke apart, and we all gasped as we saw the grim limb. The leg was twice as small as the other leg, the muscles had disappeared, and the skin was buried beneath a carpet of black, wayward pubic hair. I would have run away, but my leg was too weak.

"Oh, dear," muttered my mother. "Do you think the dark cast caused all that hair to grow? I read in *Reader's Digest* that strange things can happen like that."

The doctor looked at me and noticed my panicked expression. He winked.

"Sometimes hair does grow without reason," he said with authority. "This will probably be gone within a few days."

He was correct. That hair disappeared before morning. The mangy mess almost clogged the toilet, but I shaved it off and limped to bed. Dr. Scheele passed away several years ago, but I often think of him and smile.

My continued blossom on the youthful tree of life was not attractive. I became a near-sighted, left-handed, gangly, goofy girl with wrinkly hair and absolutely no ability to conform. Outside of farm chores, the only activity for youth in the farming community of 1,000 was a program called 4-H. The organization for youth was led by adult volunteers who promoted the four personal areas of focus: head, heart, hands, and health. Desperately hoping to help me focus and find some element of usefulness, my mother enrolled me in a 4-H cooking class with the admonition that I behave and not embarrass her. I failed on both assignments.

Twelve pre-teen girls enrolled in the 4-H club, and the leader, a doctor's wife, had the meetings in her home. I usually sat on the floor so I wouldn't disturb the meticulous décor. The couches were covered in bright floral chintz with coordinated fabric covering the matching side chairs. Festive garden-themed wallpaper featuring red velvet roses covered the walls, and pictures of pastoral scenes hung in gilded frames. A carved clock ticked softly on the polished marble mantel. I still had traces of manure on my shoes.

Each club member was required to do a cooking demonstration, and I practiced at home for weeks before it was my turn. I wasn't thrilled about the assignment to make a lemon cake but I had promised my mother I would do it. I assembled my recipe, ingredients, and supplies and reluctantly stood in front of the group.

"Elaine will now complete the demonstration for a delicious cake," the leader said as she read from her manual to the group of wiggly girls. "Pay close attention to her technique and remember that we can all learn from this effective method as we increase our attentiveness and observe problem-solving procedures. Someday, you will have the privilege of cooking for your own family."

I donned my hand-stitched apron and carefully positioned my pre-arranged supplies and ingredients on the kitchen counter.

"You must use a sturdy, large bowl for this batter," I said, feeling wise and competent. "And a wooden spoon is necessary for proper mixing."

I dumped the ingredients into the bowl and began to stir. The leader watched intently and made serious comments on my evaluation page. A few of my friends giggled with anticipation because they suspected I would deviate from proper protocol. I couldn't disappoint them, so I added a new twist to my demonstration.

"Sometimes an added ingredient can be fun for the recipe," I said. Then I reached into my pocket, pulled out a dead mouse I had found earlier in the barn, and dropped it into the cake batter. I stirred solemnly and waited for the mayhem. Some of the girls shrieked, others covered their mouths in horror, and the rest looked at the leader for her reaction. I just kept on stirring, naively thinking I would be commended for introducing a brilliant way to spice up the dull meeting. I imagined receiving a trophy on stage at some worldwide 4-H conference.

I underestimated the leader's rage. On the verge of tears, she grabbed the bowl and tossed it into the back yard, knocking over one of her prized begonia plants. I could see the tail of the little mouse sticking up from the batter. This wasn't my finest hour. I realized I probably wasn't ready to have the privilege of cooking for my own family. And I definitely hadn't improved the group's head, heart, hands, or health.

The leader called my mother and demanded that she immediately get me, and I was ordered to stand outside and wait. A few minutes later, my beleaguered mother maneuvered the station wagon in front of the house and rushed to the door. She didn't look at me, and she suddenly seemed older. As my mortified mother offered profuse apologies to the leader, I slipped into the back seat of the car and tried to be contrite. I heard the leader yell that I was never allowed in her house again and that I was kicked out of the 4-H club. Forever.

I guess that was the first time I got fired. I never did retrieve our nice, heavy mixing bowl. My mother was humiliated and refused to consider the humor in the situation. I still feel bad about the incident because it caused her shame within the community. The next day, I was sent to the potato field to pull sunflowers but I didn't mind because I was more comfortable there than in a room with velvet wallpaper.

With one simple rule, my diligent parents instilled a desire that made me hungry to work: no work, no dinner. While employed as a child on my father's farm, I weeded potatoes, hoed sugar beets, and moved sprinkler pipe. I often dreamed of the jobs I would have after I grew up, scraped the mud and manure from my boots, and moved into civilization.

There weren't many female role models for me to emulate. All of my teachers were females, and I liked them, but I didn't want to deal with students who acted like I did. The only other working women in the small farming community were two nurses, several hairdressers, a few bank tellers, and some waitresses. Those professions were noble and necessary, but didn't attract me. I wanted something different.

In addition to owning the farms, my father owned a trucking company called Montana Express. The business became successful when my father discovered an amazing new invention during the 1960s: frozen TV dinners. He leased a truck and began hauling frozen food throughout the Northwest, and soon our freezer was stocked with aluminum trays of Salisbury steak, mashed potatoes, peas, and apple crisp.

He soon leased seven more trucks and begged his friends to help drive. Hauling food and household products came with side benefits. Any time a pallet was damaged, his customers wouldn't accept the delivery so he brought the shipment to our home. We had gallon jars of capers, crates of Clorox Bleach, boxes of assorted soup, and pallets of toilet paper. We were a mini-Costco before Costco was in business.

I remember the determined look on my mother's face when my father would appear with another load.

"Look what we have here, Leona. Enough canned lima beans to last for years!"

"That's nice," she would say as she positioned several TV dinners into the oven. "Thank you so much."

I was in school before I realized meals didn't come packaged on frozen trays. I was amazed that fresh food actually had delicious taste. I always knew that mushy meat under the sloppy, brown gelatin didn't come from Salisbury.

By age eleven, I was tired of doing chores around the house. I watched my dad's industrious activities with the trucking company and asked him to get me a job in transportation. He arranged for me to have a newspaper route. Every day I saddled up my one-speed bicycle and delivered seventy copies of *The Twin Falls Times-News* to people in Wendell, Idaho. There were only seventy people in the town who could read. These daily adventures provided a small income and fostered my ability to chat with anyone.

Unfortunately, my route gave me a lifelong fear of dogs. They would bark when I got near, chase me, and bite my legs. There was one huge collie that would run up, place his big hairy paws on my shoulders, shove his head in my face, and snort with putrid bad breath. However, the experience was positive because it prepared me for my future dates at the University of Idaho.

I gave up the newspaper route after one bitterly cold winter. The snow was so deep, I had to push my bicycle from house to house. The route took two hours, and by the time I stumbled home, my clothes and nose hairs were frozen. I was too numb to cry. Buck Edwards, a crabby old man at the end of the route, called my parents and complained that I had been late with his Sunday edition. The next day, I sneaked some raw hamburger from my mother's refrigerator, mixed it with my dad's cigarette ashes and some raw eggs, rolled the concoction into Buck's newspaper, and wedged it behind his screen door. When I got home, I called the newspaper and quit the job. I accepted the fact that I was no longer eligible for sainthood.

That first employment experience encouraged me to seek greater opportunities, preferably inside. One day in junior high school, my friends Sandy, Jeanie, and I were talking during lunch break. We analyzed our lives and determined not to waste our enormous potential.

"I want five children," Sandy said.

"Well, I'm having ten!" exclaimed Jeanie. They looked and me and waited.

"I want to travel the world and write books."

They stared at me with wide-eyed amazement. I scrambled to justify my desire.

"Have you seen the pictures in *National Geographic?*" I asked. "Don't you want to see another country?"

"That's silly talk," Sandy said. "Who do you think you are?"

I thought about her question as I finished my lunch, wadded the paper sack, and tossed it into the garbage can.

"I'm just a goofy girl from Southern Idaho. But, I'm not staying here just to have babies and work on the farm."

They laughed at me, and we hurried to class. Decades later, Jeanie was the mother of ten children, and Sandy had five. Both were still married to their first husbands. In contrast, I had two kids, three marriages, and I had visited 32 countries, written several books, and worked in management jobs. Our pre-teen aspirations had come true, and we were relatively happy without any felony convictions or outstanding warrants for our arrest. That was the true mark of success for children who grew up in the village of Wendell.

The world seemed to turn faster after I reached my forties. My children grew up, moved out, got married, and started to have kids of their own. Soon, my children and I were the same age. One day my active five-year-old granddaughter came over to help me bake a cake. After covering the entire kitchen with flour and dirty dishes, she took a bite of batter and said, "We should throw a mouse in the batter and see if Daddy finds it." My legacy shall continue.

~

The Great TV Blooper of Southern Idaho

My first full-time job resulted in a live television experience that caused farmers across southern Idaho to run outside and look into the northern sky for an obscene image. I'm profoundly grateful that the event occurred before the public knew how to use the Internet to permanently record my humiliation.

In May of 1973, I packed all my worldly possessions into my Pontiac Firebird, inserted a John Denver cartridge into the car's eight-track tape player, and drove away from the University of Idaho with the idealistic enthusiasm of a college graduate who believed she could do anything and everything. More than four decades later, maturity and truth have tempered the exuberant optimism, but the outcome has surpassed my original expectations. The reality has been painful, liberating, and rewarding. There are more checks in the plus column than in the minus column, so I'll take that as proof I didn't screw up the entire experience.

I was confident I could get a job. I had a degree in journalism, graduated with Phi Beta Kappa scholastic honors, and the country was wallowing in the Watergate scandal. I wanted to be the female version of Bob Woodward and Carl Bernstein, the famous journalists from *The Washington Post* who wrote about Watergate and received inside information from a clandestine informant named Deep Throat. Their reporting led to the resignation of President Nixon. I was confident I could be just as influential.

My full tank of gas wouldn't take me all the way to Washington, and I was limited on funds, so I drove 450 miles from Moscow to Twin Falls, Idaho to begin my esteemed career in journalism. I stayed overnight with my parents who lived thirty miles away from Twin Falls, and I nodded politely as they questioned me about the facts that I had neither a job nor a boyfriend. I wasn't worried. My father offered me a job in his massive farming operation, and I declined. We were both relieved.

During the last week of May, I wore my best polyester blue dress with a white collar and drove to *The Twin Falls Times-News.* I proudly carried my resume bulging with tear-sheets from my published articles and copies of writing awards, and walked into the front office prepared to begin the job immediately. Looking back, the naiveté was comical. I didn't have an appointment, an in-house mentor, an internship, or a clue. My only previous experience had been writing for the university newspaper and a semester as an intern writing obituaries for *The Lewiston Tribune,* a small newspaper in northern Idaho, in exchange for three college credits. I hoped the newspaper officials had forgotten that nasty incident with my newspaper route many years earlier.

"You'll need to take a typing test," the receptionist said after I completed the job application. I eagerly agreed because I had typed volumes of term papers on my portable manual typewriter, and I was a fast typist. She led me to a workstation but I cringed when I saw an IBM Selectric typewriter, the kind with the typeball that rotated and pivoted with each letter. The machine didn't have a moving carriage return because the typeball and ribbon moved from side to side automatically. I felt like a 21-year-old dinosaur.

I sat down, looked over the assignment, and started to type. My left hand kept reaching for the non-existent carriage return, the whirling typeball distracted me from completing each word, and the electronic sound was nothing like the familiar clacking of my manual typewriter. The stopwatch sounded before I was half finished with the assignment. I flunked the typing test.

The receptionist smiled briefly and encouraged me to apply again another time. I hugged my portfolio, walked back to my car, and realized the ramifications of being unemployed. I had no money and nowhere to live, except at my parents' home. Four years of college and an exemplary resume were negated because of an electric typewriter. I turned on the car and John Denver was singing "Sunshine on my shoulders makes me happy." I turned off the music and drove away.

After driving aimlessly for a while, I headed to the east side of town and turned onto Elizabeth Boulevard. There it was, an outdated, flat-roofed, ramshackle white building with huge red letters that read KMVT-TV. The local television station pulled me in like a lost child. I parked, gathered my papers, and marched into the building.

"I want to apply for a job," I told the receptionist. She had two pencils stuck into her beehive hairdo and she smelled of Avon's "Unforgettable" cologne mist. My mother had the same perfume in a pink bottle with the gold collar and had used it only for special events since she received the gift in 1960. She never attended too many galas while down on the farm, so the pretty bottle remained full and fragrant on her dresser.

The receptionist peered over her reading glasses.

"There aren't any secretarial positions open now, but I can take your application."

"I'd like to apply as a news reporter," I said, blinking back the tears from my eyes. Her perfume was potent.

After a painfully long silence, she spoke.

"We don't have any openings right now, and we've never had a female on the news team."

Those two facts should have sent me out the door, but I had a vision of living with my parents for the rest of my life and smelling like "Unforgettable" cologne mist as I rocked on the front porch, a knitted afghan in my lap.

"Could I interview with the news director?" I asked, mentally scrambling for any reason to get beyond the gatekeeper.

I could tell by her negative expression that she wanted me to go away. I turned to leave and bumped into a man hustling into the building. He smiled and I noticed his nametag: Dick Tuninga, News Director. It was now or never.

"Hello," I said, offering my hand. "Could I have just ten minutes of your time for an interview?"

He was in a good mood and invited me to his office. I felt Perfume Lady's eyes burning holes in my back as I followed him down the hall.

The newsroom had three metal desks beneath a bank of flickering television sets. Assignments were scribbled on a blackboard on the wall, and piles of video tapes and papers covered a battered credenza. The nearest television station was one hundred miles away in Boise, and this was the best news department in southern Idaho.

Mr. Tuninga was shorter than I was, so I hunkered down. He moved a box of supplies from the only guest chair and asked me to sit. I did.

"What brings you here?" he asked, hoping for a personal interview that could bring him some publicity.

"I want to be on your news team," I said and offered him my portfolio.

He looked disappointed.

"Well, we don't have any job openings, and..."

"And you've never had any females in the news department. But, I promise you will never regret hiring me."

He seemed amused by my cocky attitude and picked up the resume. After reading several pages, he looked up and stared at me. I stared back.

"Have you ever been on live television before?" he asked.

"Yes," I answered. It wasn't a lie. When I was five years old I had been a guest on the children's show on KMVT with the host named Happy Holly. In college, I had concentrated on print journalism and had taken only one required class in radio-television but had never participated in a live interview or telecast.

Another man entered the room and Tuninga introduced me to J. J. Alexander, the other person on the news team. He was short, too.

"This little lady wants to work with us," Tuninga said.

Alexander stared at me in the same manner as his boss, and I returned the look.

"We could be the first in Idaho," he muttered. "Boise doesn't even have a full-time female news reporter."

That was my hook. For once, my gender was an asset. I worked it.

"It's time you had a female on the air. I know the community, I have a proven portfolio, and I'm a good worker."

I could tell their main focus was to beat the Boise markets. I could have been a female one-eyed pole dancer, but I didn't care. I wanted the job.

They led me into the studio and told me to read some copy in front of the camera. I performed like a pro. They introduced me to the General Manager Harold Hirte, and he echoed the same sentiment. "We'll be first." I nodded with conviction. I would lead the tiny station into glory and prestige.

He offered me a full-time job and said the station could pay $450 a month with a raise in three months. I shook his hand and agreed. The job would begin the next day.

I floated to my car, began driving back to my parents' house, and pushed an Elton John music cartridge into the tape player. He sang about sitting on the roof and kicking up the moss. I sang along at the top of my voice, "How wonderful life is when you're in the world." The title was "Your Song," and this one was for me.

My job as a television news reporter and talk show hostess at KMVT-TV created a unique experience as a public celebrity. The station was the only option in southern Idaho, and the nightly newscast attracted more than 25,000 avid viewers. Twin Falls was not a major market, but it was my start in business. I was only twenty-one, but everyone knew me, and there was no anonymity when I walked into a public establishment or event. I couldn't wear sweatpants at the mall, forgo makeup on weekends, or grumble while waiting in line at the post office. Even my gynecologist wanted to chat about my television show during exams. I can still picture his face bobbing between my parted knees as he quizzed me about the opportunity to appear as a guest.

My role model was Jane Pauley, just a year older than I was. She had recently started her career in television news in Indianapolis and eventually became the co-host of *The Today Show* on NBC. I followed her career and admired her spirit.

The men on the news team often reminded me I was the first female newscaster, and I needed to look polished and professional at all times. Somehow I still needed to earn my right to be employed, while the men resembled scruffy hobos when off the air. Being fashionable wasn't easy when almost half my income was allocated for rent, car insurance, and utilities. But I was young and ambitious, so I learned how to mix and match clothes, add simple accessories, and avoid wearing white on the air. Television adds pounds anyway and light colors turned me into a talking blimp. I also avoided my favorite turtlenecks and scarves because they made my head look like a hairy bowling ball perched on an animated pile of disheveled laundry. For all this glamour, I worked fifty hours a week and received $450 a month.

I wore the favorite polyester, navy-blue and white pinstriped dress with a white collar until it fell apart. Other inexpensive clothes included a black pantsuit worn with solid color blouses and a long blue jacket with tan pants. I attempted to tame my frizzy hair after some viewers called the station to suggest I needed a different style. The men could wear a dark suit every day and sport the same hairdo for ten years and no one noticed.

I had joined the ranks of young women in television in a profession previously dominated by men. I could feel some resentment from politicians and community leaders when I interviewed them on serious subjects. Their doubt made me work harder, and I slowly gained the respect that the male reporters took for granted. Sometimes I received assignments from the news director that challenged my ability, so I crawled onto a potato harvester in a dress, traveled to film and report on a fire in the middle of the night, and sat through mind-numbing city council meetings with hour-long debates about mundane issues. But I did it, much to the news director's surprise and approval. After a few weeks, even Perfume Lady at the front desk greeted me with a smile.

Only one month after college graduation I was holding a microphone and interviewing Idaho Senator Frank Church. For the first time in my life, my parents no longer referred to me as the Problem Child. Instead, I became the television personality they personally had molded and supported from birth. The blinking red light on the top of the live studio camera became intoxicating with its power.

One harrowing news assignment still makes me queasy. I traveled in a helicopter with Senator James McClure, a nationally recognized leader in energy and natural resources. Our job was to tour wilderness areas in western Idaho in support of the senator's campaign to preserve the Hells Canyon National Recreation Area. In addition to interviewing the senator, I also filmed the excursion with an old Bolex camera. I had no formal training in filming, but had learned by watching the other newsmen. As the helicopter took off and rose straight up, I pointed my camera out the window and began filming.

That's when I learned about vertigo and nausea. The erratic motions of the helicopter combined with the focus on filming made me nauseous. I blinked back tears and swallowed hard to quell the disruption from my stomach. Suddenly the helicopter lurched and I lost my composure and my lunch. A ghastly stream of soupy vomit spewed from my mouth onto the senator's expensive trousers. For one brief but terrifying moment, our eyes met and there was no affection between us. Only puke.

"Throw me out," I begged, dropping the camera and wiping my mouth with the skirt of my favorite blue dress.

The senator and his assistant grabbed some tissue paper and attempted to clean up the mess. The co-pilot tossed back a towel and I buried my face, wondering if I should play dead. The stench in the small craft became overpowering, and I vaguely remember hearing the pilot announce that we needed to head back. It seemed to take five years to return to the airport.

I rushed to my car and drove to my apartment where I threw away the dress, climbed into the shower, and sobbed like a baby. Tossing a dead mouse into a cake batter demonstration was excusable as a youthful indiscretion, but vomiting on a United States Senator was not included in my job description. I returned to the television station without the camera or my pride.

Years later, Senator McClure and I became good friends. He excused my outrageous conduct and said he'd seen worse behavior in Congress. He also joked that I'd given new meaning to his memory of Hells Canyon.

The station management forgave my gaffe and for an additional challenge decided to give me a live talk show called "Our Changing Community." The only problem was that nothing ever changed. Twin Falls was an agricultural community of 30,000 people and the liveliest discussions included the sewer bond issue, the high gasoline prices, or the current price for potatoes.

I was the host and producer of the thirty-minute, live program that appeared twice a week. I've always been unorganized; a trait I like to think is a sign of creativity. In reality, I'm a slob. I haven't seen the top of my desk for ten years. I write memos on sticky notes and lose them. I buy organizational folders and containers, but stuff them with unpaid bills, articles I'll never read, worn golf socks, and candy bar wrappers. The crumbs on my office floor proved that the station didn't have mice.

My messy and chaotic habits damaged my ability to effectively produce my talk show. Because of our small staff, I also had the producer's responsibility to invite and keep track of the guests. I usually forgot who was coming or lost my notes. This lack of planning made for some interesting shows. One time I double-booked a school choir and some local politicians. I quickly interviewed the politicians and during the commercial break I helped set up the risers for the choir. After the show, one of the politician's wives called the station to complain that her husband wasn't given enough airtime, so I rescheduled him for another time. Other times, when I couldn't find any guests and it was the night before the show, I called former high school buddies to come over and be the guests. We made up topics, and no one ever questioned the program.

Back in those days, I didn't have a team of assistants to help me. On assignment, I drove the company car, found the person I needed, set up a huge camera on a tripod, turned it on, and walked in front of the camera to do the interview. After the job was done, I turned off the camera, loaded everything into the car, drove back to the station, and unloaded and processed the film in a dark room. Then I edited the film, took it to the engineers, wrote the script, and read it on the air. I learned all of this on the job.

While doing standup reports outside in the winter, my nose would run. More than once, I needed to turn off the camera, blow my nose, and start over. Another time I accidentally gave the engineers the wrong film to air during the news so as I was describing the upcoming crusade by the Reverend Billy Graham, the audience saw my footage of a woman's reproductive system I had filmed during my interview with a local health official. The station received several complaints about that newscast.

Besides reading the news and hosting and producing the live talk show, I also was the Weather Girl. Yes, they called it the Weather Girl because Weather Woman was too formal and sounded like a comic book character. At the small station, there was no need for a meteorologist. I ripped the current weather reports from the Associated Press Wire and read them on the air while standing in front of an antiquated map of the United States. I made up most of what I said, and no one ever knew the difference. What do you expect for $450 a month?

My horrible, obscene blooper remains one of the all-time mistakes ever aired in the history of television news. The local farmers were tuned in to hear the weather report because it was harvest season and they feared a looming rainstorm could damage their crops. Before a commercial break, I teased on air that I had important information about the weather so everyone should listen. I knew the audience anticipated my big news.

After the commercial break, the red light flashed on the studio camera and the cameraman cued me to start talking. I was breathless with anticipation. Here are the words that came out of my mouth on live television:

"Important news. We have a *fold cunt* coming in from the north."

I froze. The cameraman fell onto the floor. The engineers stomped their feet in the control booth. The news anchors grabbed their stomachs and fought laughter. My mind scrambled and all I could imagine were thousands of people running into their yards and looking to the north.

"I don't see it. Where is it?" They would exclaim.

I noticed the switchboard light up with outside calls, probably from shocked and outraged dignitaries, so I did the only thing I could do. I pinched my thigh until it bruised and kept talking as calmly as possible. I explained about the pending *cold front* and how the changing weather could impact the crops. After the weather segment was over I waited for the commercial break and ran to lock myself in the bathroom. I didn't come out until the news was over and most of the staff had gone home. I was sure the on-air profanity tied with the horror of vomiting on a senator.

The station received several complaints and there was one threat from someone who wanted to notify the FCC to have the license suspended due to obscenity. However, the station manager also heard many comments from grateful viewers who said they needed a laugh. Unfortunately, this blooper is not preserved on tape. That's probably for the best, but some of those farmers are still outside searching the northern sky.

~

What if Arts Patrons Acted Like Sports Fans?

During my early reporting career, I covered sports events as well as community arts productions. I love musicals, plays, and literary readings because there's something elegant about dressing up and going to the concert hall to hear the local philharmonic orchestra or watch talented artists sing and dance or buy books from new authors. The sporting events were noisier, smelled worse, and required less thinking, so I began to compare and contrast the two activities.

The diversity between the games and the glamour became obvious after a family holiday dinner when the menfolk migrated to the TV room to watch an NFL football game. I listened to the growls, shouts, and exasperated complaints and howling coming from the guys as they became engrossed in the action. I waited for a commercial break, strolled into the room, and quietly suggested we watch a musical instead so they wouldn't be so distressed. They grabbed the remote control and glared at me like angry toddlers.

"We're having fun!" they exclaimed. I backed out of the room, properly chastised. They already knew it would be inappropriate and useless to ask me to return with beer and chips. I retreated as they began to holler about the referee's questionable ancestry. Their boisterous, emotional investment in the game inspired me to ponder about different audiences. What if patrons of musical and artistic productions expressed the same emotions as sports fans?

I can imagine the philharmonic orchestra warming up before the classical performance of Rossini's "William Tell Overture." The concertmaster enters, expecting polite applause, but the audience whistles, cheers, and throws popcorn. The oboist plays the tuning note and the orchestra solemnly responds with their respective instruments. A guy in the back of the concert hall blows an air horn.

"How do you like dem horns?" he hollers, much to the delight of the other spectators.

The conductor enters with great fanfare and bows to the audience. People in the front row wave huge foam batons and chant, "Go, Maestro, Go!" He mounts the podium and raises his arms.

"Touchdown!" someone yells. The crowd guffaws and snorts. Several call for the ushers to throw them a beer.

The music begins and the orchestra performs with controlled passion and splendid talent. Suddenly the first chair violinist accidentally fumbles her bow.

"You missed a note!" someone yells. "It's right there on the page. How could you miss it?"

Someone stands and yells at the orchestra, "We want an instant replay!"

"Send in the second chair violinist!"

Mayhem ensues until the flamboyant trumpets quiet the crowd with a commanding call to action as the orchestra charges triumphantly into the overture's finale.

"Hey, that's the theme to *The Lone Ranger!*" someone shouts. "Will he be here for half time?"

"No, that's the music they played during the orgy scene in the movie *A Clockwork Orange.* Dude, that was weird!"

Another patron stands and hollers, "Where are the Indiana University pep band and cheerleaders? They perform to this song at every basketball game."

The finale ends with a flourish of crashing timpani drums, resounding cymbals, and blaring trumpets. Once again, the guy in the back stands and blasts his air horn. The crowd jumps up and yells "Bravo!" Some excited fans rush to the stage and dump a champagne ice bucket on the conductor's head as their rowdy mates explode with a cacophony of laughter, belches, and farts. The orchestra members run to the dressing rooms.

The media wait patiently for the conductor to emerge for the news conference.

"What do you think about that prelude?" a concerned reporter asks. "Do you think the five solo cellos gave it all they could?"

The conductor blots his forehead with a silk handkerchief and slowly returns it to the pocket of his long-tailed tuxedo.

"We practiced all week for that section," he says. "Did you hear how superbly the timpani rolls resembled distant thunder? We couldn't have done it without the teamwork and dedication of every player performing in unison."

Another reporter shoves a microphone in front of the conductor. "Is it true that you're about to be replaced by a younger conductor?"

"Goodness gracious, no." he replies. "The board just renewed my contract, increased my salary $1,000, and bought me a used Buick. I'm committed to this orchestra!"

Outside the concert hall, a gregarious group of fans meanders to their favorite bar, the "Arts-R-Us Cantina," to plan their next artistic adventure. Multiple screens are showing various performances from around the world: musicals, dramatic readings, stage plays, several concerts, modern dance ensembles, and a new production from a college Shakespeare Theatre. The fans hoot and cheer after every solo performance and dramatic reading.

"I hear the ballet is opening next weekend," one exclaims. "They have lots of pretty women dancing around in skimpy dresses."

"Yes!" another one exclaims. "I read that the show is called *Swan Lake*. Maybe I'll bring the huntin' dogs and my shotgun in case there are some ducks to shoot."

Conversation turns to their fantasy arts leagues.

"My pianist won Most Valuable Player and is scheduled to perform in the *Andy Williams Show* at the prestigious Moon River Theater in Branson, Missouri!"

"Wow, you're lucky! My trombone player fell off a hay truck and broke his arm. He's out for the season."

"My understudy actor was moved into the lead position for the next performance!"

"I acquired a painter who finished more projects than any other artist in the entire division!"

"My opera singer secured the lead in *The Barber of Seville!*"

The entire group stands, raises their fists, and sings, "Figaro. Figaro!"

After the post-concert analysis, these dedicated Fans of the Arts acknowledge the late time on their Salvador Dali melting clocks, wipe the crumbs from their "I Love Bassoons" sweatshirts, don their franchised ballet mufflers, zip their commemorative Mark Twain Lecture Series jackets, and pick up their official Pirates of Penzance pennants.

"See you at the next concerto!" one says.

"Don't forget the hotdogs and caviar canapés."

The last one out the door turns off the lights. Wistfully thinking of his hero Charles Dickens, he pronounces his closing soliloquy to an empty room.

"It is a far, far better thing that I do, than I have ever done; it is a far, far better rest that I go to than I have ever known."

He tosses his empty beer can into the garbage, adjusts his private parts, belches, and closes the door. He pats the heads of his patient dogs waiting in the back of his pickup truck and drives down the road as the scene fades to black.

~

The World Can Kiss Our Attitude

We never decided what to name our group of six middle-aged women friends. Suggestions varied from "Six Pack" to "Six in the City" to "We Were Seven but One Died." Every time we met, we would vote on a new name, but we couldn't agree so we stayed with the "Midlife Happy Hour Club."

"That's so boring," Kitty said. "Can't we add something sexy?"

"How about that waiter?" Linda replied. The joke was old, but we were, too. We clinked our glasses, savored the martinis and wine, and settled into a familiar pattern of camaraderie. We had promised Pam, the one who died from breast cancer, that we would carry on without her.

"Chop them off now so you won't get sick!" She'd whispered at the end, as we took turns pressing ice chips onto her lips. We nodded in solemn agreement.

"And promise me you'll all stay friends. Keep laughing. You don't need boobs to laugh."

Over the years, the Midlife Happy Hour Club gathered regularly to acknowledge the fact that life sucked so we should laugh hard. The agenda varied, and we could grow equally passionate about politics, religion, nail polish, or the best stool softener. Sometimes we placed a glass for Pam.

One memorable occasion was to celebrate Linda's birthday. Such annual affairs often took a wicked turn as greeting cards turned into cruel and unusual punishment for still being alive.

"I'm weary of birthday cards that mock seasoned women," said Debby. "Over the hill, my ass. We couldn't climb a hill taller than a plate of cookies even with sturdy tennis shoes and an industrial crane."

We agreed and vowed to stop sending each other stupid, insulting cards. Unless, of course, the card included a lovely photo of fit, shirtless dudes in cowboy hats. We're shallow like that.

A flock of perfect women tittered past on heels that cost more than my first car.

"Look at her," laughed Debby as she adjusted her don't-give-a-shit matronly body. "She's so skinny if she swallowed an olive it would show in front and back. I should stab her with a fork to make sure she's not a poster."

Linda, the birthday babe, gasped with feigned indignation. "I read that some women are paying for a fake butt. Can you imagine making your behind bigger on purpose? I can see mine even when I walk forward, and I didn't pay a dime extra for it!"

"Stop," Jennifer said with mock chagrin. "At least we don't have periods anymore and can wear white pants without worry."

"Ha!" I retorted. "The last time I wore white pants my grandkids told me to hold still so they could show a movie on my butt."

We giggled and snorted with middle-aged abandon. We loved the glamorous gals, we really did, but our biggest consolation was knowing they were growing older, too, and would someday arrange their own midlife happy hour. By then, we would be watching reruns of *The Carol Burnett Show* and reading salacious novels in big type. We would live together in a quaint cottage near the park and pool our savings accounts to hire off-duty firemen to rub our feet. It was a glorious plan.

Kitty bit into a carrot cake muffin smeared with enough cream cheese frosting to adhere a Buick to the wall. "Mmm," she moaned. "I just eat this for the vegetables."

"True," I agreed. "And this medicinal lemon drop martini has just enough citrus to cure my scurvy."

We ordered a second round before the end of Happy Hour to have the two-for-one deal. The conversation turned to hot flashes, ailing parents, and future birthday parties. Nancy had one too many cocktails and began moaning and groaning about turning fifty. I finally got tired of her complaints and told her to pull up her control-top, big-girl panties and get over it. When she continued to bemoan the fact that her gumption had no function, I asked if she would prefer to drop dead at age forty-nine. The question caused her to ponder a suitable answer.

"I can't die yet," she muttered as she sat up straighter and tossed her chemically treated blonde bob away from her face. "The mortgage is almost paid off, and there are still several boxes of Girl Scout cookies in the freezer." We agreed she should stay alive.

Linda, remembering her birthday, sniveled through dramatic sighs that she was so insignificant she could stand naked in the middle of town with her hair on fire while dollar bills flew out of her saggy butt and no one would notice. For her, age fifty was a dark symbol of physical and mental deterioration.

"That's aging," I said. "But don't worry. I promise to notice if dollar bills fly out of your butt."

We sat silently for a few minutes as we sipped our drinks. Kitty finished her muffin, licked her finger, and said with sugar-fueled authority: "Let's evaluate the facts so we can stop the pity party and get on with a raucous celebration of life."

Kitty described how we should deny that our prime time was over, and we should refuse to become Norma Desmond in the old movie *Sunset Boulevard*. True, our skin wrinkled like a pricked balloon, our perky boobs had morphed into pendulums somewhere around our waists, dot-to-dot spots appeared on our arms, hair turned thin and gray, and after we waved at someone our arms continued to flap for five minutes. Our volatile intestines kept us guessing if we'd be constipated for a week or running to the bathroom every hour, and we exercised regularly just to maintain the weight we didn't like. We endured hot flashes, mood swings, hairy toes, and forgot our keys while caring for aging parents and rambunctious grandkids.

"What's not to love about this reality?" she asked.

"But wait, there's more!" I said. "We also get to be the fodder for jokes about menopause, mothers-in-law, and incontinence, while crotchety, old men are revered as distinguished and successful."

"Somebody order another round," said Kitty.

"And the cheese plate," Linda suggested. "And some chocolate."

As we nibbled and noshed, we talked about the true advantages of aging past fifty. After the kids grew up and left home, the empty nest meant less laundry, lower meal expense and preparation, and no more frantic nights waiting up for them to come home. We didn't need to purchase tampons anymore or lock the bedroom door to enjoy a spirited romp between the sheets. We played with our delightful grandchildren and sent them home. We had more time to pursue hobbies and lovers, volunteer, travel, and read books. The hair on our legs grew lighter so we didn't need to shave every day. And, we had the power to throw away all the silly "Over the Hill" birthday cards and party favors. For us, being over the hill meant we got to tumble down, laughing all the way.

"There is nothing you can do about aging," Debby said as she plucked an olive from her martini and dangled it over the glass. "If you were born during or before 1966, you're approaching or over 50. That's how it works, and there are no exceptions. Unless you die." She plopped the olive into her mouth and licked her lips.

"We should celebrate that we're living resource manuals," I said. "We existed before cell phones, personal computers, microwaves, social media, instant rice, and tampons. The younger generations can learn a lot from us."

"Don't say another word!" Jennifer halted the conversation and grabbed her purse. "I gotta pee. Who's coming?"

Two others slid off their chairs and the threesome paraded to the restroom chattering and chuckling until they were out of sight. I've always wondered why women couldn't go to the bathroom alone, but that was a dilemma to examine another day. I snatched the last piece of cheese before the potty party returned.

"I need to leave early," Linda said as she reached for some money to pay her tab. "I've got a hot date with a cool guy to celebrate another birthday. We may skip the dinner and just chase each other around the room until one of us falls down. That's our version of foreplay."

"Remember when we were so stressed about being perfect, having the right lover, raising stellar children, and making sure our purses matched our shoes?" I said. "Such bullshit."

"Youth is overrated," Nancy said. "Really, would you go back to your twenties or thirties? I'd love to look like I did, but I don't want to relive the challenges, heartache, worries, and exhaustion of those years. I'll stick with being feisty at fifty."

We toasted another productive meeting, drained our glasses, and called for the check. Happy Hour was over until the next time, so I stood to leave and was sideswiped by a petite ingénue with a gigantic designer bag. The luggage didn't leave a mark but it bruised my ego.

"Excuse me," she muttered as she plowed her way to the table where the cool kids were sitting.

"No worries," I replied. "But you could plow snow with that maneuver and that suitcase."

She ignored me, and I was ready to rumble until Linda tugged on my arm.

"Let it go" she said. "She's just a mosquito at our picnic."

After forty years as an administrator for a major university, Linda always knew how to soften any potential angst. The mosquito analogy was perfect.

"Are you going to yoga in the morning?" Linda asked as we waited for a cab. We participated in a gentle class for women over fifty, and the most difficult maneuver was getting up from the mat on the floor.

"I need to go because I missed the last class," I said. "I was so tired my downward-facing dog had to be put to sleep."

"No excuses," she said. "See you in the morning."

We waved goodbye and I plopped into the cab that would take me home. During the ride, I thought about the daunting designer bag. It reminded of an article in *The New York Times* that described the unbelievable lives of women who marry rich men and live in the Upper East Side in New York City. The article caused tongues to wag faster than a group of over-privileged kids on a playdate at a lollipop factory. The author let her pinky finger down long enough to write exaggerated, torrid tales of year-end bonuses paid to the women for excelling at their wifely duties. I missed that memo and married for love.

At least paying the little woman a bonus is better than killing her and substituting a robot, per *The Stepford Wives.* Sometimes I think the wealthy husbands would prefer androids so they could avoid and eliminate all that messy relationship drivel. I also suspect that some of these women will be promoted to The First Wives Club after their bored husbands find younger, prettier, more efficient models to replace them.

The must-have purchase from these pay-to-play marriages is a Hermes Birkin bag that costs around $120,000. That's not a house; it's a purse. As does my sensible, inexpensive, black tote bag, a Hermes treasure will hold tissues, assorted combs, lip gloss, a few pens that work, a wallet of worn credit cards, crumbs, and lint. I win.

The article created quite a commotion among my online group of middle-aged friends. Comments ranged from "Pricey Prostitutes" to "I get my designer bags on sale" to

"Where's New York?" After reading about how the hyper-scheduled children of these arranged marriages need counseling to learn how to play, I threw up my hands and my breakfast. I decided to turn the designer tables and offer my own counsel, gleaned after more than five decades on this amazing planet. I don't need a Wife Bonus, but I'll gladly give a regular gratuity to my husband.

After I arrived home, I wrote down some suggestions for a blog about how to give a Husband Bonus:

Arrange weekly adult playdates. There is no need for counseling when you remind your lover that there's a party for two tonight at nine o'clock. Toys and finger puppets aren't necessary but could come in handy.

Show your private equity fund. Sleep naked and receive a robust return on your investment.

Don't wait until yearend for a bonus. If you're both older than 55, take advantage of the time you still have. There is a good chance you'll be asleep long before midnight on New Year's Eve.

I will never own a purse that costs more than my first house. A designer bag is just an empty container of stale air. I promised my sweetheart that I'll never pine for anything fancier than a fine Cabernet. I'll offset the request with a gift certificate for a couple's massage. See how this works?

The New York Times article stoked the flames of indignation, jealousy, and insecurity among many readers. When the dust settles, the rich wives will have their cleaning women come over to tidy the mess, my friends in the Midlife Happy Hour Club will continue laughing at life, and I'll fix a cheeseboard and cocktails for the patio and invite my husband to join me. It's time for a bonus with benefits.

~

Stay Relevant and Thirsty, My Friend

My friend Nancy and I were waiting patiently in line to exchange the bling-covered, thigh-high boots we bought in a moment of unbridled foolishness. There may have been alcohol involved with the purchase.

"If this line goes any slower, I'll have to chew these boots for my dinner," Nancy said.

"Tell me when cobwebs begin to drape from my ears," I said. "I think the warranty just expired on my new tires."

"Oh, look! I think the sales clerk just noticed us and gave a faint smile."

"We must appear cloistered as a huddled, nameless clump of middle-aged humanity humbly seeking assistance," I muttered. Women around us nodded in agreement, and some were nibbling on their packages while others stood cross-legged in a desperate attempt to halt the pending explosion of body waste all over the floor. Most of us would rather wear adult diapers than leave a long line just to go to the bathroom and return to the end of the queue.

Then a young tart with a plastic face and noisy bangles came skittering up on her six-inch heels, shoved her assets in front of us, and received immediate attention from the animated sales staff. After being ignored, the crowd of gentle, older women disregarded their childhood instructions to be people-pleasers and began to channel their dormant inner sorcerer.

"We could curse her until she spontaneously bursts into flames," I said.

"No, if we have that much power, let's turn her older than we are."

The group cackled like possessed magicians. Nancy felt emboldened and moved closer to the counter.

"You must be so much more important than I am," she said. "My mama told me not to be pushy like you, so I'll just continue to wait here looking at your imperfect backside."

She added a toothy smile, raised her eyebrows, and tilted her head ever so slightly.

The intruder felt the glare of angry eyes on the back of her well-styled hairdo and turned around. Sensing a pack of wild women who were hungry, breathing their last breath of tolerance, and in need of a bathroom, she stammered an apology and slinked away before the sales clerk could call for security. We high-fived like silly school girls and pushed toward the counter. Nancy and I managed to exchange the boots in time to return to the shoe department before the store closed.

Nancy knew that it was improper to verbally assault a stranger in public, thanks to that unfortunate incident a few years ago at Home Depot. She was wrangling a cart of spray paint to the checkout when a tiny, young, self-absorbed woman hustled to the front of the line, hitting Nancy with an oversized furnace filter.

"Watch where you're going, PeeWee!" Nancy said as she pushed the box out of her face.

"Take a chill pill, Grandma!" the busy woman said between snaps of her gum.

Nancy turned brighter than the color chart in the paint department.

"You need that filter for your mouth, Sweetheart!" But her irritation didn't stop with the witty retort. She grabbed a can of spray paint from her cart, tore open the top, and sprayed metallic gold paint, the designer edition, onto the young woman's filter and high heels.

That's when the manager intervened, escorted Nancy from the store, and told her never to come back. She had to drive across town to another store to get her paint, but she smiled all the way.

A few days later, it was time for another meeting of the prestigious Midlife Happy Hour Club. We selected a local watering hole to imbibe, laugh until we almost wet ourselves, and solve the problems of the world.

Jennifer, known for being vocal and indiscreet, is the most unoriginal. She's worn the same hairstyle, told the same stories, and had the same husband for thirty years. She always orders a Zinfandel even though we encourage her to try real wine. On very rare and special occasions, she'll be sassy and order a martini.

Debby, the divorced fashion queen, can't wait to be a grandmother. She's at the point where she doesn't care that her grown children aren't married. Debby was the first in the group to learn how to wear a scarf a dozen different ways, and she spent an hour teaching us how to do it. We humored her and some of us almost choked ourselves.

Kitty, the overworked caregiver, cares for her ailing mother and babysits her grandkids twice a week. She's offered to give them to Debby. She has an appetite for life, food, and drink and continues to believe in her mother's admonishment to always clean her plate. Forever on a diet, she has gained and lost the weight of a well-stocked refrigerator. Her second husband is a fireman, and he's on call with his job as much as Kitty is with her mom and grandkids.

Nancy, the part-time yoga enthusiast and full-time pastry lover, is my hotheaded friend. She loves crafts and can turn a broken table from a yard-sale into a fetching piece for the living room. Her favorite mediums are spray paint, designer duct tape, and salvaged pottery. She used to make ceramic ash trays but smoking became taboo so she removed the indentations and calls them soap dishes. Her husband is a pharmacist, and he likes her to wear his white coat around the house with nothing underneath. She's not shy about sharing risqué information, and we vacillate between irritation and wanting written instructions.

Linda is the most successful businesswoman of the group. She has an impressive title and people return her phone calls. Sometimes, when we're getting more boisterous than usual, she'll discreetly slip on dark glasses and look around the room to make sure her staff members aren't in the area. She's the one most likely to sneak peeks at the cell phone. We fine her $5 every time.

I am the group's resident wino, hopeless romantic, and storyteller. Someone needs to do it.

A recent discussion focused on creating a list of helpful tips for how middle-aged women can be bold without being bitchy.

"What's wrong with bitchy?" Debby raised the question as she raised her glass. "No one tells me how to behave."

"That's what your ex-husband learned the hard way!" responded Jennifer.

"I think women need to be more self-assured when they are in public situations," I said. "A busy sales clerk doesn't have the time or desire to interact with a person who is docile, soft-spoken, and projects an image that she's not worthy of anyone's time."

"That was my mother!" Kitty said. "She never spoke up for herself, but she still moaned about being ignored. She took the experience to the Martyr Level. After a while we called her Saint Serenity of the Holy Church of Submission."

"Don't you think that was the customary behavior during our mothers' time?" I asked, remembering my own timid mother who wouldn't complain about an imperfect meal in a restaurant and never returned an unwanted blouse to the store. In her mind, she deserved less than what she received because she was unworthy. Bless her heart.

"So, how can we encourage other women to remain relevant without being a bitch or a martyr?" Kitty asked before ordering another martini.

First of all, we agreed that women should act as if they own the place. A confident attitude combined with good posture and assertive language sets the tone for a positive experience and rewarded expectations. We don't intend the music to stop and people to stare when we enter a room, but we will arrive with gusto and not sit in the back.

Conversely, a cowering, insecure approach won't receive any attention, except from creeps who exploit women's vulnerabilities. We've all experienced those jerks. By now I can smell these guilty goons from across the street, and they stink.

"Shine without shame!" exclaimed Jennifer. We clinked glasses in solidarity.

Second, we agreed, women should look beyond the cliché that says they must love themselves first. A woman shouldn't adore herself if she's a notorious bitch, too lazy to remove last week's makeup, and dresses like a truck stop hooker. She should cultivate mannerisms, talents, and attributes that make her appreciated in a world of other women who don't give a shit. Her example should make the most calloused critic admit she has redeeming qualities and should be noticed.

"I need one of those ambush makeover attacks," I said. "Last week I made a quick trip to the grocery store and was wearing a rumpled 'I Love Beer' t-shirt and flannel pajama bottoms. I met ten people I know, including a member of the city council."

"That happens all the time to me, too," said Linda. "I always wear a scarf just so I can twist it around my neck and appear fashionable."

"I don't wear scarves because of that nasty incident with the elevator door. I almost strangled myself," I said with great sadness.

Nancy endorsed our opinions. "I love my yoga pants and flip-flops, but I'm wearing diamonds and Spanx to the symphony!"

Linda continued the discussion about how to remain relevant after fifty. After five decades, a woman has survived the angst and fragility of youth, the frantic responsibilities of careers and raising children, and the added demands of caring for aging parents and addressing their own health issues. By then, women aren't just worthy of simple recognition but deserve a sparkling crown and boisterous parade down Main Street. A marching band would be a nice touch. A tray of gourmet chocolates and expensive wine delivered by a silent stud named Thor would be even better.

"But what if some of us aren't as bold as the others," Kitty asked while caressing her wine glass. "You might think I'm insecure but I'm just quiet."

"Then boost your energy, Sweetheart," Jennifer said. "If you want to be unseen, that's your choice. But if you want to be recognized as a breathing human that matters, you need to assert a positive, distinctive aura."

"I'll try to adjust my aura," Kitty replied. "Perhaps I'll focus on an attitude of distinction."

"But what if you're confident, dressed well, and smiling and the world still ignores you?" Nancy asked. "There comes a time when I just say *screw you!*"

"Hear, hear!" I cheered.

We looked around for a waiter to bring another round of drinks, but couldn't catch anyone's attention. Nearby tables of young men and women were loaded with full drinks filled by attentive staff.

"Guess we're invisible," muttered Debby.

"Let's do an experiment!" Jennifer giggled. "Watch me."

She stood and left the room, reentered, and stood in the middle of the room for several minutes. Waiters jostled around her as they brought food and drinks to the other tables. Then she whispered to one of the young women at the next table and they left the room. The young woman, a gorgeous, tall beauty wearing an obscene dress, entered the room and stood where Jennifer had been standing. Two waiters, one male and one female, rushed over and eagerly asked if they could help her. Jennifer slipped her a five-dollar bill and returned to our table.

"I offered her five bucks to prove a point," Jennifer said proudly. "She got attention and I didn't."

"You wasted money on that?" Nancy snorted. "Give me five dollars and I'll dance on the table and sing an opera. That'll get a reaction!"

The waiter finally arrived and took our orders.

"Sorry for the wait," he said. "It's been busy this evening."

"Remember, we tip better than the young gals do," Nancy said.

He took notes and hurried away.

"You know," said Kitty, "sometimes women don't *want* to be the center of attention. When women are secure in themselves, recognition is nice but not necessary." She sat back and sipped the last of her Zinfandel.

"You're correct," I said. "But we're at the age when we finally know what we want, and it's fine if sometimes we choose to be alone and other times it's perfectly splendid if we want to sing out loud and dance in the street. We want to make that choice for ourselves, and we're not ready to be forgotten. We will not become irrelevant."

Kitty looked thoughtful for a moment, then stood and yelled across the restaurant to the waiter, "I'd like a martini, extra dirty!"

~

Why Your Children Are Cute but Should Move Out

My neighbor appeared at my door early one morning with a plate of warm scones.

"Get the coffee," she said with an eager grin. "We're celebrating."

I was apprehensive about the pending conversation because I knew she was having trouble with her children and grandchildren living with her. The home was roomy, but not adequate for eight people in three generations for four years. Over coffee and buttered scones, she told me the reason for her joy.

"We're selling the house!" she exclaimed.

"But it was your dream home," I said. "What about the kids?"

"I'm tired of fighting. They won't leave. We've offered to help them get an apartment, but they don't want to move. After all these years, our grandkids think it's normal to live with us. I just want to walk naked into my own kitchen."

"Well, that's an image I didn't need," I said. "But it's too bad you have to move because your kids won't."

"The house was too big, anyway," she said. "We're downsizing and we'll have only one spare bedroom for occasional guests. We're so excited!"

After my neighbor skipped back to her soon-to-be former house, I poured another cup of coffee and thought about the issue. According to national statistics, more than three million twenty- to thirty-four-year-olds live with their parents, the highest number since the organization started keeping records in 1996. Several online groups and resources, such as AdultChildrenLivingatHome.com are available for parents seeking guidelines for handling the situation. Reasons are varied: tough job market, horrendous student loan debt, inability to buy health insurance, expensive housing, the parents enabling the situation, and the adult children's reluctance to take responsibility. Perhaps we should take a lesson from nature and watch adult birds push the babies out of the nest.

One of the big advantages of getting older is that your children eventually grow up and move away. For some reason, when my kids turned eighteen they ran out of the house as fast as they could, kissed the ground, and mumbled something about "Free at last!" But after lengthy therapy sessions they now visit occasionally, and that's a good thing. They even let me watch their kids, after I pass a fifty-point checklist and agree to security cameras and Breathalyzer tests.

After the last one left for college, I turned his room into the guest room. I didn't want to appear too eager, but his stuff was boxed and in the garage before his car hit the city limits. I finally had a place to dry laundry on the bed, cram bags of unread mail into the closet, and ignore the cobwebs that looped from lamp to window like delicate lace décor.

I was thrown into a panic when I knew guests were coming to spend the night. I gathered clutter into garbage bags and tossed them into the garage where they languished for months. I frantically dusted and was amazed at the true color of the furniture. Once I used a vacuum hose to capture the cobwebs, but I accidentally sucked up the curtains and broke the rod. After that, I just waved a towel around and hoped to catch the webs before the evil spider sought revenge and jumped up my nose.

I enjoyed sharing time and space with my children and friends, but there is an important rule when having houseguests: Don't make it too comfortable. If you include little dishes of individual, scented soaps, a collection of salacious books, and a small refrigerator stocked with wine and cheese, expect them to set up residence and never leave. You'll have a problem when they forward their mail to your house. That's a bad thing.

We love our adult children, but we don't want to enable them to squat in their former bedrooms. Don't keep their rooms as they left them. Some of my friends still have the stuffed toys, artwork on the wall, and frilly curtains and bedspreads from the Hello Kitty or Strawberry Shortcake eras. Box everything now, donate the usable stuff, and toss the junk. You might give your child a week's notice, but that's sufficient. Otherwise if Sissy is having a horrible day, she'll rush to the comfort of her old room. Unless you turn off the electricity and take in a band of gypsies, she could be there for a few years. It's better to hold her, offer emotional support, and enable her to work out problems on her own. Besides, her old room would make a great wine cellar.

Remind your children that you, too, once were poor as a church mouse and your parents didn't offer free room and board. That's because they also started with nothing. It's part of life, and only rich kids with trust funds don't have to struggle during their young adult years. Most of us started with bean bag chairs, boards on cinder blocks for bookcases, and a fifteen dollar per week grocery budget. That's why we appreciate our homes now, and we don't want our children to have them, yet.

I've plotted some devious strategies to encourage adult children and guests to bid adieu and seek other adventures. I don't care how cute or fun they are, there comes a time when I want to be alone to sprawl on the couch in my underwear, munch on cookies, scratch my belly, and watch reruns of *I Love Lucy.* Many guests don't want to participate in this scenario, but if they do, there are other ways to reclaim your home.

Be a horrible cook. I enjoy preparing and serving delicious meals for company, and they tend to enjoy the treatment and expect it every night. I'll fix one or two special dishes, but after that, it's pizza and chicken nuggets. Guests are welcome to take me out for dinner, but young adults think a gourmet burger joint is fine dining. I don't want to go anywhere that offers balloons for the kids or weary waiters singing the happy birthday song.

Play obnoxious music throughout the house. The Six Fat Dutchmen Favorite Hits collection is a raucous blend of jaunty Polka music that is guaranteed to irritate even the most sedentary, comfortable guest. After a few repeats of "The Beer Barrel Polka" your adult children will claw their way to the door and stumble down the street. Mission accomplished. Backup choices include western music by the forlorn, harmonizing Sons of the Pioneers or anything by the Bee Gees. Be sure to sing along in an off-key falsetto. Experiment with other horrible music and keep notes for successful selections. Other adults will beg for your list.

Infestation can discourage even the most comfortable guest. Leave a few dead bugs on the kitchen table and set some mouse traps in the guest bathroom. Warn guests to wear shoes and watch out for varmints. Sneak to their room in the middle of the night and scratch on the closed door. Leave a badger trap on the front step for extra dramatic impact.

Channel your inner vixen. Accidentally leave packages of condoms on the counter and mutter to yourself about "getting lucky tonight." Be sure to pound on your bedroom walls and moan loudly all night. For inspiration, watch and reenact the orgasm scene from *When Harry Met Sally.* With luck, your guests will be out before breakfast.

Get political. Fix your television sets to only show political programs that your young adults can't stand. Regularly talk about your allegiance to candidates they hate. Remark that you cashed in your retirement funds to send to the most obnoxious candidate. Enjoy their shock and awe.

Get religious. Play spiritual music and dance around the house chanting while you scatter charms and crystals. Don't forget to wear a flowing robe and sit on the counter to meditate. This option comes with unexpected negative consequences because your young adults may want to join you. In that case, revert to the Six Fat Dutchmen.

Grow old in front of them. Stare at your adult children for a long time and ask them to repeat their names because you just can't remember. Your young adults want you to remain young and helpful, and they can't deal with the role reversal. They're not ready to take care of you. Pat them on the head and tell them to go be independent while there is still time.

These are just a few recommendations for dealing with the postponed empty nest. If these suggestions don't work, you may need to take drastic measures and move away. That worked for my kids.

A week after my neighbor floated from my house, another friend called asking for advice. Her twenty-six-year-old daughter had lost her job and wanted to move back home so she could get "back on her feet." I suggested that my friend write a contract for them to negotiate and sign.

"A contract?" she asked. "You're kidding!"

I explained to her about some research I had found after hearing about my neighbor's dilemma. I listed the bullet points.

Why is your child moving back home? If your adult child has gone through a tough divorce or lost a job, it's natural for parents to want to help. However, if they want to play video games in the basement, eat all your food, and expect you to do their laundry, that's not right. If they bring their lover, pet, and/or soccer team, that's your fault for making stupid decisions.

Don't count on an oral agreement. Your child may ask to stay a month but take years to find a job and move. In the meantime, you'll get resentful and frustrated and could potentially harm the relationship. Sit down with him or her and write the list of guidelines and expectations. That will show how important the issue is to both of you because a written contract also keeps a record of the terms. If you wrote that Junior can't bring his collection of boa constrictor snakes, and he does, you have cause to show him and his slithering menagerie to the door.

Write who will do what. If your grown daughter is old enough to dye her hair fuchsia and party like a rock star, she's old enough to do her own laundry, clean up the house, contribute to the grocery fund, and make pleasant conversation. A contract will outline the duties and include charges for rent and utilities. Susie won't get on her feet if she's never paid for rent and you're doing all the cooking.

Don't forget the exit plan. If you're lonely and need the companionship of your children, it's okay to have them visit and stay sporadically. That doesn't mean they can move in and hope you die soon and leave them the house. Write down the date they are to leave, and then sign and date the contract. It will give you some leverage when Buddy refuses to budge.

The best rule is one of hindsight. Establish the expectations when children are young, and remind them that they will grow up, leave home, and survive. Keep the lines of communication open, and enjoy their progress. Some day you may need to move in with them. Remember that they learned from you, and be wary if they play songs from The Six Fat Dutchmen.

~

My Feminine Mystique Sprung a Leak

I attended elementary school during the sock-hop days when my role models were stay-at-home mothers and June Cleaver of the television show *Leave It to Beaver.* My teachers were female, and the principals were male. During the 1960s, girls in high school were required to wear dresses, take Home Economics, and learn how to bake snickerdoodles. Boys followed orders to take shop, get greasy, and belch in the lunchroom. There's nothing negative about those early mentors, but I thought the guys should also learn how to cook while the girls should understand why cars needed oil changes. And without a doubt, everyone should enjoy a good belch.

Our movies and music followed the same regulated pattern. *Dr. Zhivago* portrayed the dramatic story of a man in love with his wife and another woman. A reverse scenario wouldn't have been accepted. *The Sound of Music* became the highest-grossing film of the 1960s, and I loved the sass and songs of the main character, Maria von Trapp, played by Julie Andrews. Based on a true story, the woman's life was complete after she married the authoritative captain and cared for his children. I didn't know any captains.

Our early understanding of sexuality was confused as we matured. Our favorite television show, *I Love Lucy,* portrayed separate single beds in the married couple's bedroom. Girls in the late 1950s fell asleep listening to their transistor radios as Elvis Presley crooned, "Are You Lonesome Tonight?" By 1963, we were "wishing and hoping" for a boyfriend as Dusty Springfield told us to "Wear your hair just for him. Do the things he likes to do." Then Lesley Gore sang "You Don't Own Me," and Nancy Sinatra advocated a new wave of feminism with "These Boots Are Made for Walkin.'" It's no wonder the sexual revolution began and thousands of free-love, freeminded females danced in the mud at Woodstock.

Fathers weren't questioned as they enforced their complete authority over the household while their submissive wives admonished the offspring to obey or just wait until your father gets home. Punishment for disrespectful behavior caused me to be exiled to my room where I spent most of my childhood as penance for my stubborn attitude. The entire family supported my banishment because we really didn't like each other.

When I occasionally entered the family quarters, I was allowed to watch a few television shows. I assumed *Leave It to Beaver* and *Father Knows Best* happened on another planet because the fake family was so cheerful, perfectly dressed, and didn't fart at the dinner table. The episodes always ended with a positive conclusion as Ward/Jim gathered the respectful children and offered sage advice while June/Margaret smiled in the background holding a tray of cookies.

"Golly, gee," I'd say as I mimicked Beaver Cleaver's favorite line. I assumed that phrase was code for "Bullshit."

Then Betty Friedan wrote *The Feminine Mystique* in 1963 when I was in middle school and exposed the uncomfortable truth: Many women with husbands, children, and homes weren't happy.

One line in her book caused considerable hostility from traditional readers. "Gradually, without seeing it clearly for quite a while, I came to realize that something is very wrong with the way American women are trying to live their lives today."

I imagined the traditional housewife peering over the clothesline, tempted to wander beyond the white picket fence. June Cleaver secretly wanted to rip off her pearls and pawn them for a Dodge Dart convertible so she could dash off to the city to get a job as a stenographer. Other women chose to stay home and criticized the tarts who tossed their aprons into the wind and exchanged housedresses and sensible shoes for suits and stockings with seams. It signaled the beginning of the endless mommy wars.

My father rejected the early feminist theories and heartily endorsed the character of Archie Bunker from the television show *All in the Family.* I remember him laughing as an indignant Archie proclaimed, "A woman should cleave unto her husband. Right here in this house is where Edith's cleavage belongs."

My parents were strict in the guidance and rearing of their children, and they believed a child, if frightened enough, could be taught to make wise decisions. I was often given the choice of "clean up your plate or go hungry." A common rule, especially for me, was "stop arguing or get spanked." Once I asked if I could get a second opinion. That impudence didn't turn out well for me.

As a consequence of these early choices, I concluded that things were either bad or disastrous. I didn't want to obey any rules or suffer judgment for my actions, and I longed to be offered a cheerful alternative that would leave me breathless with joy.

"Hey, Elaine, we want to reward you for being such a good girl. Do you want a pony or a custom-built tree house?"

After years of dodging and weaving through the patriarchal family dynamics, I devised some clever survival techniques. I negotiated my freedom with promises to make them proud, and life became a frantic routine of overachieving. Good grades? You bet. I earned membership in the high school Honor Society. Leadership? Easy. Student Body secretary was my claim to fame. Career advancement? Hey, look Dad. I'm the editor of the school newspaper and I want to be a writer. How do you like them apples? Sweeter than potatoes, right?

These achievements didn't matter in the real world because our school was so small. There were only fifty-six students in my senior class, so I didn't need much talent to surpass many of them. But it was that early decision to prove myself to my parents that inspired me take it a step further and dream of life beyond the village. My course from there would be up to me because there were no role models for independent females.

When I reached my senior year in high school, I begged for the chance to go to the University of Idaho. Women in my family never had the opportunity to go to college and were expected to get married and find contentment in the kitchen, down on the farm. My father was skeptical.

"Dad, here's a brochure about the University of Idaho. I want to go."

"Why?"

"I want to study journalism and be a writer."

"Why?"

"Because it's a job I can do."

"You write for a high school newspaper. Big deal."

"Dad, I'll work to earn money during the summer and on Christmas and Spring Breaks."

"Go paint the fence down at the pig barns and you can use the profit from the next sale of pigs. That will help cover a semester."

"Thanks, I'll do that," I answered. "And it will be a lot cheaper than what you're paying for Tom at Harvard."

"Your brother is male."

"Big deal."

"You're grounded."

"Big deal."

That went well. But after I received a small scholarship, my parents couldn't say no. I packed my best flannel jumpers, white blouses, and wire curlers into a blue metal trunk and marked the days until the eight-hour drive to the university.

No one talked as my parents drove me to college. I sat in the back seat of the sensible Buick Riviera and stared out the window as we left Wendell and passed lush fields of potatoes, corn, and sugar beets. Harvest would begin in two months, and for the first time, I wouldn't participate. The landscape turned to high desert and the only green vegetation fringed the Snake River as it cupped southern Idaho on its way to the Pacific Ocean. We traveled through Boise, the capitol city, and I stretched my neck to see the tall buildings and the capitol. In 1969, the population of Boise, the state's largest city, was only 75,000. We followed Highway 55 north of Boise, and the two-laned road entered a scenic panorama through the Payette National Forest, a vast expansion of rugged, timberland that spanned 2.3 million acres. The land was bordered by two of the deepest canyons in North America—the Salmon River Canyon and Hells Canyon. Our journey continued north as the road hugged the mountains along the tumbling Payette River and we climbed to 5,000 feet above sea level. I felt as if I were being born.

After five hours of driving, we stopped in the resort town of McCall and found a quaint restaurant. We were only three hours from our destination, and my anticipation was palpable. We sat in silence. I wanted to talk about moving away, but I didn't know what to say. Part of me wanted to jump up in the restaurant and holler "I'm free!" but I didn't want to blow my chances. Any disruption in proper protocol could cause my father to change his mind and take me back home where I would remain grounded forever. Deviating from my normal behavior, I kept quiet.

We left McCall and passed a pristine alpine lake. I made a mental note to live on the lake someday, a dream I fulfilled twenty-eight years later. The late afternoon sun danced on the golden grain fields of the Palouse as we neared Moscow, home to the University of Idaho. We found the new student dormitory and some cheerful students rushed out to greet us. They took my blue trunk and I eagerly followed them into the building. I never looked back, and my parents drove away. My grand adventure had just begun.

I arrived at college prepared to experience life beyond my hometown of 1,000 people. My first taste of freedom involved Budweiser beer and a clumsy frat boy. I still blush with the memory. College during the 1970s introduced this farm girl to hippies, anti-war protestors, demonstrators, musicians, poets, and wide-eyed friends who were just as eager as I was to test our wings. We studied, partied, gained and lost lovers, and attended a few classes. I played the guitar, sang in the college jazz choir, wore my hair long and parted, and bought flower dresses from consignment shops. This first experience with freedom changed my life, and I focused on one main goal: get a job and support myself. The first job came relatively easy, and I settled into television news reporting as if I knew what I was doing.

July of 1973 brought a decision that would change my life forever. I had always been interested in politics, often helped campaign for various candidates, and was more conservative than my contemporaries in college. My TV reporting job provided opportunities to interview various politicians, and I eagerly anticipated meeting them.

At the time, Idaho had two distinguished senators from opposing parties. Democratic Senator Frank Church and Republican Senator James McClure did not agree on many issues, but they were cordial and supportive in public and in private. They refused to act like spoiled toddlers wrestling in the mud in the expensive playpen in Washington, DC.

I interviewed both men on various occasions and respected them more each time. They shared a passion for Idaho and sponsored important legislation to protect the land and water. They're both gone, and I miss them.

Early one morning in July, I received a phone call while working at KMVT. Louise Shadduck, a respected political activist known as "The Lioness of Idaho," was the administrative assistant for Idaho Congressman Orval Hansen. She called to say she had followed my illustrious one-month career and offered me a job as her assistant in Washington DC working for the Congressman. I asked if I could call back with my decision, and she gave me a day.

This decision differed from the temporary admonishment of "clean up your plate or go hungry." This one offered the action and glamour of living and working in Washington, DC. I was tempted to accept the job but decided not to go. I loved my television experience and appreciated the chance to shine in a small town in southern Idaho near my roots. I feared that I would get lost and become insignificant going to the world's center of political power. Reluctantly, I turned down the offer.

The job at KMVT continued to provide excitement and new adventures. I interviewed a wide variety of characters, from a local group producing a live musical to a weathered rancher who proudly told me his sheep provided jobs, food, and wool for the community. He was one of the happiest men I had ever met.

One day I was bustling through the station and ran into a tall, dark stranger with such force that I dropped my news script and the pages scattered across the floor. He helped me pick up and organize the mess. Then he introduced himself as the new guy at the station. He had transferred from a television station in Salt Lake City, and was eager to learn about the area.

"I know this area," I said, trying to remain sophisticated and not drool. "Maybe I could show you around."

He said that would be fine and accompanied me to the studio. He worked several jobs at the station, either behind the camera as I read the news or in the control booth managing the commercial placements. The friendship took off, and we enjoyed each other's company. Once while I was giving the live weather report, he threw snowballs at me. It was an interesting courting ritual.

Even though I was determined to focus on my career, I fell in love. I was impulsive and too eager to make quick decisions about crucial matters that impacted the rest of my life. We decided to get married. Why not? Less than six months after I graduated from college, I was working full time and married. No career placement official could have predicted the life-changing journey I was traveling. If I had accepted the offer to go to Washington, I would not have met him and wouldn't have had our two children. But, I'll always wonder what it would have been like to mingle with the famous and infamous characters who shaped the course of the country during the 1970s.

I don't have any regrets about not going to Washington, but in the back of my mind, I always knew that Betty Friedan would have urged me to go. I decided to keep my feminine mystique in Idaho.

~

Reinventing the Wheel of Fortune

My life accelerated faster than my Firebird. I graduated from college in May, started at the television station in June, met a fun new employee in July, and married him in October. My parents and brothers disapproved of the wedding and refused to attend. They realized I got married anyway when I announced my new name on the air.

After a year, I decided I was ready to try a major market. We moved to Salt Lake City, and I was sure I could find a job. Sometimes exuberant naivety is really boneheaded ignorance. Salt Lake wasn't in love with me.

I became invisible. We found a tiny apartment and proceeded to look for jobs. Having one car limited our success, but we managed to coordinate the transportation. We both got jobs working at advertising agencies several miles apart. He would drive me to mine and then get me after work. It was emotionally painful when I finally acknowledged the reality of my situation.

I found a job working in a windowless office on the second floor of a warehouse for the Oscar E. Chytraus Company. I wrote co-op ads for dealers of Amana microwave ovens,

RCA televisions, and various kitchen appliances. Just months before I had been cavorting with senators. But there I was, trapped in a warehouse in an industrial district with no transportation to escape during my lunch hour. So I used the time to search the job ads in the newspaper with the intention of reinventing myself.

I found an interesting notice for a job at the University of Utah in the admissions office. The responsibilities included public relations, writing, and speaking skills. I completed and mailed the application. After two interviews, I was offered the position of Assistant Director of School Services for the University of Utah, the first female to hold the job. I was twenty-four years old.

The University was a forty-five-minute drive from where my husband and I lived, so it became apparent that I needed a vehicle. We purchased an old, beat up, bright orange Ford pickup truck, and that's what I drove to work. So no one would see it, I arrived early and parked in a distant lot and walked to my office. My office. I had a separate office and a secretary. I wanted to thank the Oscar E. Chytraus Company for motivating me to get off my gloomy butt and chart a new path. Of course, before I left Chytraus I used my employee discount to buy some appliances and a new television. Hear me roar, indeed. Nothing says success like being able to buy a Harvest Gold refrigerator.

I remember the night my career ambitions were postponed. During a business trip to Logan, Utah in 1977, I woke in the night because of a fluttering feeling in my body. I was alone in a hotel room and it was the first time I felt my baby move. That was before instant pregnancy tests, but I knew. The truth frightened and exhilarated me. I had always wanted children, but I was unsure what would happen next. After my meetings, I drove back to Salt Lake City and scheduled an appointment with my obstetrician. I was instructed to pee into a plastic cup and call back later for the results. The wait was frustrating but there was no other choice. Finally, I received the call confirming the pregnancy. I celebrated by eating a package of cookies.

It was time for the fall statewide tour of high schools, and I would be carrying boxes of brochures, audio-video equipment, and talking with high school students. I would also be carrying a baby. The thought made me tired.

At the time, I was slender so I quickly showed the pending pregnancy and needed new outfits but there weren't any clothes for pregnant working women. This was Utah where most women belonged to the Mormon Church and were expected to stay home and have babies. All I could find were cute t-shirts with an arrow and words that declared, "Baby on Board!" These maternal shirts weren't appropriate for a business environment. I finally found two empire-waisted dresses and wore them every other day for five months.

During the seventh month of pregnancy, my eyes began to bother me at work, so I gave up contacts and wore glasses. I felt like a nerdy whale. When my vision became too blurry, I made an appointment with an ophthalmologist. He studied my eyes and immediately scheduled surgery at LDS Hospital in Salt Lake.

"You have several holes in both retinas," he explained. "They must be fixed now or you will go blind."

I was panicked at the thought of never seeing my baby. My husband took me to the hospital and I was hurried into surgery. Usually, the patient is unconscious for laser surgery on retinas, but because I was pregnant, I refused any anesthetic. The doctors proceeded with caution.

LDS Hospital incorporated teaching courses with its surgeries. A group of interns was standing around the operating table and I could hear them discussing the procedure of using lasers that would fuse shut the retinal holes. My eyes were propped open with tools that resembled the cage on a champagne bottle. I remember wishing I had some real champagne to calm my nerves, but then I remembered I was pregnant. If I couldn't stone the little bugger with anesthetic, I really shouldn't get the wee tyke drunk on booze.

My head was immobilized by what I imagined as padded vice grips on both my temples. I hoped the technician wouldn't over-adjust the contraption and make my head explode. Bright lights seemed to pierce into the back of my skull, and the surgeon moved in so close I could see his nose hairs. He smelled faintly of Old Spice aftershave.

Using what looked like a long, thin spoon, the surgeon began manipulating one eye and I felt it being moved in the socket. A machine hovered overhead, ready to zap and seal the offending holes. The sensation became too much to bear, and I began to feel queasy. *Don't you dare,* I silently warned myself. It was too late. With a sudden explosion of projectile vomiting, I sprayed myself, the surgeon, and the equipment. He jumped back, not amused. I didn't care. He should have known that pulling out my eyeball would have been distracting, to say the least.

As the nurses cleaned up the mess and disinfected the machine, I remember the interns discussing if I puked because of the queasiness from having my eye moved or because I was pregnant. I was too weak to tell them to stop analyzing my barf and maybe give me a sip of water. Then another intern said I was lucky I didn't aspirate and choke on the vomit. I wanted to give him the evil eye, but both eyes were still propped open in an unnatural death stare. "Fix the damn eyes," I muttered. They glanced at each other and wrote notes.

After the surgery, my eyes were bandaged and I was taken to the recovery room. I stayed for two days in the hospital, completely blind, hooked to a catheter, and wondering if I would ever see the tumbling baby moving around inside of me. I decided to definitely exploit the drama throughout the child's life to remind her or him just what sacrifices I made. I would embellish the story with great details just to earn gratitude and devotion.

My mother came from Idaho and she took turns with the nurses and my husband to feed me. They were all clowns, those guys.

"Here comes some green beans," my husband would say. In reality it was mashed potatoes. It was so unnerving to prepare for one taste and have it be another.

"I'm lying here blind and pregnant," I moaned through the potatoes. "How can you tease me when all I want is a stupid bite of beans."

"You would do the same to me," was his response.

"No. I would add nails to the potatoes," I answered. I wasn't the most gracious patient.

The time came for the great unveiling. The surgeon, surrounded again by note-taking interns, started to remove the bandages. I blinked in the harsh light. The blurriness was gone, and I could see. I felt let down because there wasn't any spiritual or symphonic music, but I managed a grateful smile. In a few months, I would see my baby.

I returned to work full-time, pregnant, wearing glasses, and craving chocolate chip cookies. I never again fit into the white suit with the cobalt-blue vest. At the first of March, I left work on maternity leave, intending to return. A girl, my daughter, was born a few weeks later. She scrunched her face, peeked at me, and fell asleep on my chest. I knew I wouldn't return to work in six weeks. Instead, I took a five-year break to work on my new title: Mother.

Getting back into the workforce brought me new opportunities.

"I'm here to apply for a job."

"Do you have young children?"

"You can't ask me that question."

"I only wondered because you have spit-up on your shoulder."

The job applicant screener was trying to be funny, but I got the message. I had to try harder to get hired after being unemployed for five years. At age 31, I decided to reenter the work force after staying home with my children; my daughter was almost five and my son was two. We had a mortgage on a tiny house, two car payments, and were struggling financially under the normal expenses of a young family. I knew it was time for me to return to work not only for financial reasons but because I wanted to continue my career. I polished my resume and dug through my closet for something other than sweat pants and stained t-shirts.

I soon discovered I was the worn-out lioness and the parade left town without me. The young, single, childless women with business degrees were my competition. They were hungry, driven, and didn't have stretch marks. They wore high heels, short hairstyles, tiny Austin Reed suits, and carried luggage-sized leather briefcases. In the ten years since I had graduated from college, these females had acquired the confidence to gallop up the corporate ladder without bringing coffee to their bosses. I was jealous, terrified, and determined to stay in the race.

An eclectic assortment of interviews followed. Several businesses wanted me to intern for free, and another promised "exposure" in lieu of a livable salary. The local television stations weren't hiring, but suggested I try again in a few years because the female anchors in Boise tended to stay and look the same for decades. After a few months, I got discouraged. My children were my main priority, but I knew they would need clothes, braces, and music lessons. I wanted to provide those necessities. I also was getting tired of wearing the same clothes for the past five years, the furnace was broken, and I no longer spoke in complete sentences. I needed income and a career that utilized my skills.

I spotted a tiny ad in the newspaper for a communications specialist for a regional bank. I tailored my resume to sound more businesslike and mailed it to the bank. I was feeding my kids lunch when I received the telephone call. Immediately, my two-year-old son began to whine, so I threw cookies at him. The man on the other end of the line asked nervously if everything was okay.

"Of course," I replied, sounding pleasant and composed. Portable phones weren't in homes back then, so I was tethered to the land line while I continued to toss cookies, raisins, and crackers at the toddler and his five-year-old sister. They quietly gobbled their prizes.

"Can you come in tomorrow for an interview?"

"Yes," I chirped, frantically plotting childcare, clothes, and strategy.

After finalizing the time and location, I hung up the phone and hugged the kids.

"More cookies," they begged. I obliged.

Again I bribed my neighbor to watch the kids so I could go to the interview. The bank was thirty minutes from my home and as I drove, I mentally calculated how I would manage a hectic schedule. Despite the daunting logistics required for arranging child care and maintaining the home while keeping the marriage, I had a positive feeling about the job.

I walked into the interview and immediately recognized an old friend from college and he greeted me with delight. As much as I wanted to think I would be recognized only on my credentials, I was happy to have "a friend at the factory." He was the only one conducting the interview and he immediately offered the job.

I worked in the corporate headquarters for Idaho Bank & Trust. The executives and members of the board of directors were all men. They regarded me as a casual curiosity and often asked how I contributed to the bottom line.

"I'm an expense," I would reply. "But, I'm also an asset." That line always worked.

Life for young businesswomen during the late 1980s was complicated because we had few role models. The challenge was to design our own rules and become mentors for younger females. When opportunities for advancement didn't exist, we created them. We ignored criticism from men and women and used our brains to break glass ceilings.

Sometimes all we received in return was a headache, our hair full of glass, and a hand on our ass. But, we never quit.

My next job was with Boise Cascade, a large forest products company headquartered in Boise. My career wasn't without mishaps and pratfalls. On a visit to a company facility in Minneapolis, Minnesota I slipped on the ice and severely sprained my ankle. The attending doctor filed a worker's compensation claim and my boss was irritated because it damaged our department's safety record. After that, I only traveled to Minnesota during warm months. Another time, I was scheduled to interview an executive in Washington, DC. I got lost and we never met face to face. Under deadline, I conducted the interview by telephone, wrote the story, and never told anyone that I flew across the country to have a phone call.

Flying on the corporate jet also came with tall tales and secrets. Once I flew back from the Portland office to Boise and the only other person on the jet was a tall, beautiful, young woman in a miniskirt and sheer blouse. I learned later from the pilot that she was a high-priced escort flown in by a senior vice president. I often flew to New York on the company plane and the rules changed if the chairman of the board were on the plane. He always sat in the back near the only toilet and he didn't like to be bothered. It became a professional challenge to avoid using the restroom on the four-hour flight to New York, so I avoided the complimentary cocktails just so I wouldn't have to go.

I once interviewed the corporate pilots for an article in the employee magazine. Off the record, they shared sordid stories of love affairs and illicit liaisons that occurred on the company airplanes. I can honestly say that I was never involved in any such inappropriate dalliances, but it does explain why the pilots were paid huge salaries to keep their eyes focused outside the plane.

In the fall of 1989, I experienced a career highlight. Through my office as contributions manager, I arranged for several tons of Boise Cascade newsprint to be donated to the production of newspapers for classrooms across the country. This was in conjunction with my program called "Ready to Read" that provided money for children's books. The news conference was scheduled at the prestigious Park Lane Hotel in New York City, and dignitaries from industry, education, and politics agreed to attend. The news release was timed to coincide with the company's meetings with financial analysts to review the earnings reports. I flew from Boise in the corporate jet with the chairman of the board and other executives. That was the only time I experienced the elite world of top executive travel. We landed on the tarmac at a private hangar where a limousine was waiting to take us to the Park Lane. The staff greeted us like visiting royalty, and there was a fruit bowl in my room! A fruit bowl!

The news conference was a success. The chairman read the speech I had written for him, and everyone politely clapped. The donation was a small portion of my annual four-million-dollar donation budget, but the company received priceless nationwide exposure and media attention. We flew back the next day, and I took all the fruit I hadn't eaten.

After flying high on my professional best, I soon crashed with a serious challenge to my parenting abilities. While I was on the business trip to New York, my 11-year-old daughter started her menstrual period. We previously had discussed what would happen and she had books, pamphlets, and supplies, but she didn't have me. She was too embarrassed to tell her father, so she handled the situation alone. It wasn't until the next month that she told me. I immediately regretted being self-absorbed in my success because I had failed in my important role as a mother during a pivotal time in my daughter's life. However, I was proud of her independence. Even at a young age, she knew how to take care of herself.

My corporate career ended a few months later when I returned to work after the New Year's holiday. The day started full of energy, and I was excited when my boss scheduled an appointment with me in his office near the end of the day. I was convinced he was giving me a raise for doing so well on the contributions programs. I reminded myself to be humble as I entered his office and sat down. But I was blindsided when he told me the company had eliminated my position. I laughed because I thought he was joking. But he didn't laugh in return.

I stared at him in disbelief, fighting the urge to use my outside voice. "What?"

His voice was monotone as he recited his memorized script. I wasn't being fired but my job was gone, so I would be transferred from my top floor office with a window to the basement and wait for special projects. In addition, a new job was opening and would be given to a woman who worked in another corporate office. This was the office version of "the other woman."

I returned to my office, gathered some personal items and my briefcase, and walked silently to my car. I knew the security cameras were recording my every move. I walked with my best corporate posture.

My husband was out of town, so I calmly fed the kids, talked about their day, and said good night. Then I opened a bottle of wine and drank it. The next day, I got the kids to school and sat in my recliner and watched old black and white movies featuring Jeanette MacDonald and Nelson Eddy. I didn't call my office to say I wouldn't be there and refused to answer the telephone. Every few minutes I would remember the shock, pain, and ramifications of losing my job. I was the breadwinner for the family, my job gave me high exposure and prominence in the community, and I loved what I did. Even though my salary would continue, I would need to sit in the basement and wait for pity projects. I was 38, and I needed to start over again.

I returned to work the following day and everyone averted their eyes as if I had a contagious disease. Even the other women, my friends, stayed away. The facilities management department already had moved my personal belongings and miscellaneous office supplies to a small windowless cubicle in the basement. I had no staff, no assignments, and no motivation. No one questioned the decision but each employee knew she or he could be next. The corporation owned the job and could give and take it away on a whim. I wore my fancy suits less often.

I lasted two months alone in the basement before submitting my resignation. I didn't end my employment at Boise Cascade on a high note.

I sent an e-mail to the executive who had been my mentor but had betrayed me. I had kept "as new" an e-mail the executive had sent me months previously praising my accomplishments. On the day I quit, I returned the e-mail with a note: "Thanks for nothing."

I sent the e-mail, took the elevator out of the dark basement, slapped my security card on the reception desk, and walked out the door into the sunlight. As the automatic doors closed behind me, I may have flashed an obscene hand gesture. My corporate days were over. It was time to reinvent myself, again.

~

Validation on a Volcano

"Hey, Mom, do you want to hike across a volcano?" My 26-year-old daughter called, almost giddy with her challenge.

"Have you been reading my life insurance policy?" I asked, suspecting something sinister was at play.

"Come on," she begged. "It's the experience of a lifetime. We'll backpack for three days across the Haleakala Crater in Maui and go from 10,000 feet to sea level."

I was sitting on my patio sipping an adult beverage at the time and considered it a major chore to hike to the kitchen to refresh my drink. At age 52, I had no burning desire to backpack across an isolated crust of earth covering molten lava and deadly gases, especially in a region that had active volcanoes. I suspected she may have been using some of the local narcotics prevalent in Hawaii but then remembered she was a health guru and the founder of an outdoor adventure company for women. She was sober and serious. I told her I'd think about it and call back.

After Emily graduated from college, I gave her a roundtrip ticket to Hawaii as a gift for obtaining honor grades. She traveled there but neglected to return. In love with Maui, she worked multiple jobs and shared expenses with various roommates to pay for the high cost of living. She worked on a tour boat, and I was shocked to learn that one of her jobs was to free-dive to the bottom of the ocean and set the anchor. No one did that in Idaho. She quit that job after diving too deep too quickly and a blood vessel erupted in her eye. That's just one more reason not to dive to the bottom of the sea without air tanks and scuba gear.

I've always avoided any temptation to dive below the surface of the ocean. I enjoyed snorkeling, but I feared at any moment a crazed shark or pack of carnivorous eels would grab me and take me to the bottom for a snack. This fear persisted when I was in swimming pools. I belong on dry land.

During past family vacations to the ocean, I encouraged everyone to jump into the water. Everyone except me.

"I'll just stay on the boat and relax," I would holler to the rest of the family as they disappeared beneath the waves and came up laughing. In reality, I was scared shitless and preferred to be in a space where I could breathe air uninterrupted. Needless to say, I never joined a scuba diving club and I needed emergency oxygen after seeing the movie *Titanic.*

During her five years in Hawaii, Emily created Abroad Adventures, a travel company for women. With her friend Jessica, she organized various excursions around Maui that went beyond the typical tourist activities. They completed the first few trips to work out any problems, and then she opened the tours to the public. She assured me the experience would change my life.

"I just want to return with my life," I said. "There's something a bit unnerving about being on a volcano, don't you agree?"

"You only live once," was the answer. "And I think you would love a three-day hike in the wilderness."

"Who are you and what have you done with my daughter?"

"Come on, Mom. I'll be right behind you on the trail. Do you think you can't do it?"

She was a clever one to bait me with that line. I had used it on her many times during her volatile childhood years. Of *course* I can do it.

After our telephone conversation, Emily e-mailed the necessary information that described the hiking trip across the Haleakala Crater. The expedition began at the visitor's center, elevation almost 10,000 feet above sea level, and crossed the southern ridge of the crater for 15 miles, coming out at the bottom of the Kaupo Gap and ending in Hana. The third day promised hot showers and long massages. I wondered if I could skip to the last day and forgo all the activities that required boots and depleted oxygen. That choice was not an option. Refusing to admit defeat, I called, signed up for the trip, and went to buy a backpack.

I had lived more than half of a century without hiking for three days, but I cautiously felt the need to score one more physical adventure before retiring permanently to the patio. The conversation in my brain proved the struggle between excitement and trepidation. The positive impulses created a cacophony of cheerleaders in my mind.

Claim the new journey. Hike across a volcano as a vibrant woman. Feel your body and soul bathed in the cool breeze from the ocean beneath a dazzling sunlit sky.

The negative imp darted between the cheers and shouted harsh, destructive warnings.

You're a fool. You're old. The volcano will erupt. You'll die.

Finally, I was weary of the battle and went to the kitchen to make a sandwich. An important decision of such magnitude couldn't be made on an empty stomach. I pulled out a bag of vegetables I had purchased at the local Farmer's Market and laughed when I read the label.

Volcanic Farms: Organic and Original.

"It's a sign," I muttered. "These fresh tomatoes from Volcanic Farms can only mean one thing. I am destined to walk across a volcano, with or without tomatoes."

The cheerleaders jumped and gyrated with joy. The pessimists left to call the next of kin.

At the time, I lived in the mountain town of McCall, Idaho. I enjoyed taking afternoon hikes in the mountains around the area and owned the proper boots, socks, and clothes. I loaded my new backpack with extra clothes and supplies and practiced carrying it on the mountain trails. The elevation in McCall was a respectable 5,000 feet above sea level, but I would be starting the Maui hike at twice that height. The night before I left for the airport to fly to Maui, my confidence began to waver. What in the hell was I doing? The phone rang.

"Hi Mom! All ready?"

"I think I have a sudden serious illness and I may need to cancel."

"Too late," she said. "We already have a full tour of eight women. And, don't forget Band-Aids."

"Band-Aids? Do we need to trap, kill, and gut our food for dinner? Are you afraid I'll cut myself with the knife?"

"No, but we're walking 15 miles over rugged terrain, and the Sliding Sands Trail is over colorful cinder rocks that can shift. You might fall and cut your leg or get blisters on your feet."

"I paid to do this?" I asked, fighting the image of tumbling on sliding cinders into a hidden vent inside the volcano only to steam to death like a hapless lobster in a pot. "How about we spend three days on the beach? We could go shopping for new sandals that will never touch a sliding cinder."

"See you tomorrow," she said. "And make sure you pack some Imodium in your first aid kit. We're bringing a lot of fresh fruits and vegetables, and you know what that does to your digestion problems."

"Don't worry," I said. "I had a lovely conversation with some tomatoes, and we're good to go."

The next morning, I walked into the airport wearing the overloaded backpack, looking like a wandering, misplaced hippie who had completed one too many trips.

"Going to hike a volcano," I proudly told the airline attendant as I checked the pack.

He smiled but didn't say anything.

"Good thing it's dormant," I said, trying to convince myself of all the pending fun and glory.

The attendant stopped and looked at me. "I hope it's not that one on Maui," he said. "I heard a guy up there was attacked by a pack of feral dogs and he leaped to his death into the ocean."

I stared at him, my face blank and shocked. Eventually he looked frightened, crouched down behind the ticket counter, and didn't budge until I walked away. As I ambled through the security line, I tried to ignore the loudest voice in my head.

You're going to die!

Emily met me at the airport with a fresh flower lei and placed it around my neck, and we joined the other hikers for dinner and instructions. There were eight women, and two guides, and I was the oldest by 15 years. We were assigned various duties, from carrying extra water to helping with tents and cooking. We shared rooms in a pleasant hotel near the ocean and were told to be ready by 3:00 the next morning.

"I used to come home at 3:00," I growled. "Can we wear jammies?"

"No. Be prepared to watch the glorious sunrise and then we'll begin the hike."

"Can I just go sleep in the van now?"

"Mom, please."

I took the hint and stopped complaining. I wanted to wait at least another day before totally irritating my daughter. What could she do? Call for a pack of feral dogs?

It was dark and cool as we loaded gear, tents, and food into a van and drove a winding road from Kahului up to the Haleakala Visitor Center. We stood wrapped in blankets and holding mugs of hot coffee to watch the sun come up over the mountains. The vision was both mesmerizing and humbling, and we felt magnificent and miniscule at the same time. Bundles of colorful clouds draped over the mountain peaks and changed in hue and size as the first rays of sunshine pierced the darkness. Steam rose as the warm light covered the cool rocks, and we were enveloped in a light mist until the sun burned away the fog and illuminated the valley and rugged canyons below us. There was no sound. I was unusually quiet as I viewed the majestic panorama and adjusted to the thin air at 10,000 feet. Such a magnificent sunrise happened every day, but only a few dedicated early risers were privileged enough to see it. Just buying the video wouldn't be an adequate alternative.

After a quick breakfast of fruit and muffins, we drove to the Halemauu Trailhead, wiggled into our fleece jackets and backpacks, and waited like excited children for professional instructions from our guides. Their advice was powerful.

"Start walking," they said.

The first posted sign indicated we were walking to the Holua Cabin, only four miles away. I looked back to the parking lot, but the van was already gone. I was trapped on top of a mountain on an island in the middle of the ocean, and the only path down was over a treacherous lava field of moving volcanic rock. I briefly wondered again if my daughter had ulterior motives. Then she moved behind me on the trail and Jessica took the lead.

"You're doing great," Emily said.

"I've taken 10 steps," I replied.

"Just a couple thousand more. You can do it."

After an hour, we paused at the rim of a deep valley, high above the clouds. Jessica told us to look back at a large rock formation that appeared from the mist and resembled the profile of a woman.

"That's the Goddess Pele," Jessica said. "Hawaiian mythology says that Pele is the goddess of volcanoes and will guide your journey."

"Can she carry my backpack?" I whispered, not wanting to cause any trouble. I adjusted the frame and wondered if I was able to continue the pace. My doubts disappeared when I felt a surge of energy and I relaxed enough to keep up with the others on the path, following the bobbing backpack of the young woman in front of me. The wee positive voice in my head came out of hiding. *Yes, you can do it.* I walked.

After three miles, we stopped to rest and drink from our water bottles. We obeyed the strict bathroom rules of the Haleakala National Park. Don't go off the path, squat over a large rock to urinate, dig a hole for solid waste, and don't leave toilet paper. The park was home to rare species of plants and animals, and it was against the law to disturb anything off the trail. The younger women didn't seem to mind, but I struggled to get comfortable with the bathroom situation. I expected a camera crew to pop up and film me for a prank show on reality television.

I dropped my backpack and propped it in the path to form a privacy shield, pushed down my moisture-wicking travel pants, and proceeded to hurry with my personal business. Something shifted in my pack and it fell against my back, knocking me to the ground. I fell on some sharp rocks that cut into my butt. I yelped and the sound reverberated through the valley, amplified over thousands of ancient echo chambers. The group stared at me while I scrambled to my feet, cleaned my bleeding backside with a wet tissue, and stuffed the tissue in my pocket. Emily applied some ointment and bandages because I couldn't see where to apply them. I had not intended to have this mother-daughter bonding experience.

"Well, you made it a few hours without calamity," she said. I smiled meekly. The echo of my cry continued to bounce around the sacred rocks.

We donned our packs and continued the hike. By afternoon, the sun became hotter and my butt hurt as I walked. I refused to listen to the voice that warned that infection would set in any minute and I would languish on the path with my ravaged derriere exposed to the elements and meandering varmints.

"We're half way to the Kapalaoa Cabin," Emily informed the group. "We're walking over loose cinders, so keep on the path."

For the next few hours, the only sounds came from our boots as we crunched over the cinders and maneuvered the trail. Otherwise there was profound silence. We entered a vast wilderness that resembled a desert landscape dotted with scraggly Silversword plants, a distant relative of the yucca. We watched Nene, a flightless goose, scamper over the ground. Ominous clouds rolled over us, and I pulled my fleece jacket over my neck and chin. The trail became steep and slippery, and I was getting tired. At one point, I was at the back of the line, and I felt a small panic attack. My legs were beginning to mutiny.

They won't notice when you fall. They'll leave you here to turn into stone and become a solemn marker on the trail for future hikers.

The weather changed quickly, and we felt muggy. I was about to holler in defeat when Jessica stopped the group for a quick break. There was no place to sit and no shade beneath the hot sun. We removed our fleeces, drank water, gobbled granola bars, and applied sunscreen and lip balm. The morning's high spirits were gone, and we were seriously focused on the mission: get to the campsite. We were almost six miles into the hike, and not a Dairy Queen, Starbucks, or taxi in sight. We loaded our gear and proceeded into the wilderness.

Finally, we arrived at the cabin, a simple wooden building without electricity or running water. The bathroom was an old, one-seater outhouse near the cabin. I remember my grandparents had a similar rendition on their farm, and that was what my mother used as a child. I made a mental note to pay the sewer bill if and when I returned home. At least in the outhouse, I didn't fall over and cut my butt.

Another hiking group had reserved the interior bunkbeds, so we set up tents outside and smoothed our sleeping bags. I removed my boots and rubbed my tired feet. The guides made dinner in a Dutch oven and cooked it over the campfire. It was the most amazing meal I had ever eaten in my entire life. Or, maybe it tasted so good because I was hungry and weary to the bone. I fell into a hard sleep, still wearing my dusty hiking clothes. I dreamed of the cool mountain trails beneath towering pine trees back in Idaho.

The next morning, I rallied and prepared for the day's journey. The guides told us we would be leaving the Sliding Sands Trail – there was boisterous applause – and trekking through more lush vegetation as we descended to 6,380 feet for our evening sleepover at the Paliku Cabin. The parched moonscape transformed into forests of ferns, tropical trees, and dense underbrush. At least our bathroom stops became easier with the help of logs covered with soft moss. A log never looked so good. By then, our ragtag group of beginning explorers had become close and didn't need the privacy we required just the day before. We often sat on logs, doing our personal business, while chatting about the various types of vegetation along the route. Such a spontaneous sisterhood probably wouldn't happen back in the city.

We arrived at the cabin after four hours of hiking and found our inside sleeping accommodations which consisted of rows of wooden bunkbeds. My feet hurt, so I pulled off my boots and noticed red blisters on my heels and big toes. I pawed through my pack, found the Band-Aids, and secured them around my feet. I had acquired a new respect for these neglected parts of my body because I really needed them. They were dirty, worn raw in places, and the heels were rough enough to etch granite, so I smothered them with lotion and promised to get a pedicure more than once a year.

After a fulfilling dinner of vegetable soup, soft cheese, and Dutch oven pie, we sat around and talked. The women named me the official Crone, a title meant to convey respect for the oldest woman.

"You represent the power of the Crone," said one of the young women who had been studying to become a Shaman, a spiritual healer. "You have an essential role in the triple Goddess, the wise woman, healer, and midwife. You signify the ancient Crone's attributes of compassion, transformation, and healing laughter."

I nodded with acceptance. Two days before that I would have given her the death stare I had made to the guy at the airport ticket counter. But that night, on the south edge of the Haleakala Crater under a domed sky bursting with brilliant stars, I was the Crone, and I had walked across a volcano and was still alive.

The next day we hiked down the Kaupo Gap and descended to 3,880 feet. The thick, humid air hit our faces as we sloshed through swamps clogged with tall grasses and over bubbling streams. We splashed our faces under a small waterfall, opened our mouths, and drank like thirsty beasts. It was the first time in my life I appreciated water more than a rich Cabernet. At the bottom of the mountain, we were met with cheerful young men driving Jeeps. One of the men was Emily's boyfriend, John, my future son-in-law. He seemed pleased and slightly amazed that I had finished the trek. I wanted him to know she came from hearty stock.

I was dirty, smelly, and exhausted, but I felt glorious, as only a 52-year-old woman can feel after she navigates an impossible journey. I looked back at the path and remembered the times I was so tired and sore, when I felt like a failure and wanted to quit, when I realized the exuberance of reaching our destination, and when I transformed from merely the oldest woman to the respected Crone. Emily had been correct. The experience changed my life. I threw my backpack into the vehicle. I haven't used it since.

The day ended at a lovely hotel in Hana that offered real beds, hot showers, and deep-tissue massages. I secretly patted the toilet with affection, acknowledging that plumbing is entirely under-appreciated. After dinner, I sat beside my daughter and we shared our thoughts about the journey. The three-day event proved to be more powerful than I had anticipated, especially since I had momentarily silenced the badgering critics in my head.

"Do you want to take a hike through the lavender fields tomorrow?" she asked.

I looked up at the dazzling stars and heard the pounding of the nearby surf. A circle of Tiki torches cast dancing figures around the fire pit, and someone in the distance was playing a ukulele.

"Not a chance in hell," I said, with all the wisdom and compassion I could muster.

~

Mom, I Joined the Army

The bond between mother and child is permanent and inseparable. Unless, of course, that darling baby boy grows up, moves out, and calls with a profound message that he's going far away where the only helicopter parent is actually flying a combat helicopter.

"Hi, Mom. Guess what? I joined the Army!"

"Wait a minute," I stammered in total shock. "Don't you need my permission?"

"Mom, I'm 22."

"When in the hell did that happen?"

I had envisioned my son Adam still playing on the floor with Legos. The trajectory from birth to age 18 seemed like an action movie stuck on fast-forward. I was wallowing in the erratic chaos of menopause and divorce combined with the raw reality of his older sister going away to college in another state. Just when I needed him most, he decided to grow up, graduate from high school, and leave for college. As he eagerly loaded his car, I raised my hand to ask one last question. "Do you have clean underwear?" But he was gone. I waited at the door, thinking maybe he would turn around and come back. He didn't.

My son and I shared similar personalities. We knew how to make each other laugh, and that's what I missed the most. He also was the man of the house beginning at age 15 when his father and I divorced. That year for my birthday, he gave me a tool box and showed me how to use every tool so I could be more self-reliant. I learned how to fix things around the house, clogged toilets being my specialty. I became proficient with an impressive assortment of wrenches, screwdrivers, and pliers. I almost ordered my own tool belt, but decided the box was sufficient.

After he left for college, the quiet settled like a sad fog throughout the house. I sat alone and wondered if I could still claim to be a single parent if no children lived at home. I was simply single. I had started over and reinvented myself so many times, I knew I could do it again. But I missed my children. Maybe I was too successful as a parent because they flew out of the nest with confident eagerness to tackle the world. Or, maybe they just wanted to get away from me. Maybe I was a horrible parent. Maybe I was overanalyzing the situation and needed some wine.

A few months later, Adam called and invited me to campus. I was packed and in the car before the telephone was cold. The drive to the University of Idaho took about four hours from my home, and I enjoyed the drive through the mountains and past the rolling wheat fields to the school. I had driven the same route as a student thirty years earlier. I started to hum the school fight song.

He proudly showed me his fraternity room and introduced me to his friends. I tried my best not to embarrass him or be too noisy. Then he loudly announced, "My mom can chug a beer and sing in Latin!" Instantly, I was held in high esteem by the gregarious men of the Delta Chi house. During a tour of the fraternity, I noticed a co-ed come out of a room wearing only a towel.

"Don't mind her," Adam said. "She showers here after class."

"Well, things have changed since I lived on campus. We didn't stay or shower at fraternities."

"Did you have electricity back then?"

Always a joker.

Later at dinner, Adam told me about a volunteer program that he had joined. It was called Camp Adventure, an educational program that enlisted college students across the country to provide leadership training and organize activities for children and youth within the community. Adam had always loved children, and even as a toddler he would help take care of sad children at the child care facility. During high school, he helped teach sports at the local YMCA, and always had several kids hanging on his back. His 6'6" frame made him a gentle giant to the little ones.

He told me about Camp Adventure and said the organization took about 10 hours of time each week. I proceeded with caution and asked if that left time to study and go to class. He assured me that he was balancing all the demands on his time. From my own past experience, I knew he could get drained and distracted by too many extracurricular activities.

The program also organized camps for children of military personnel stationed at military bases around the world. Adam had applied and been accepted to help lead the program at the US Army military base in Darmstadt, Germany.

Camp Adventure paid for his transportation, room, board, and provided money for expenses. He also earned twelve college credits. His association with the organization gave him a deep respect for the military, but his decision to join the Army came as a complete shock.

"I'm coming home next week to tell you all about it," he said before we ended the telephone conversation. "And don't worry. The recruiter assured me I would stay in the United States and not have to deploy overseas."

My courageous, positive son had acquired not only the best traits of my personality but also my tendency to believe what people told me. I had been too gullible in many situations and had lost money to ruthless scoundrels. I instantly knew the recruiter was a salesman and would say anything to get a fresh body. I told myself to remain optimistic when Adam visited the following week.

"Don't worry," he said as we shared beers on the patio. "I want to do this for the country. And the military will provide a signing bonus and help me pay for the rest of college after I get out."

I admired his conviction and bit my tongue to keep from saying anything to dampen his spirits. Silently, I worried about my spirited son becoming regulated and subjected to strict orders. I wouldn't have lasted a week.

Each branch of the military offers a skills assessment to new recruits so they can be assigned to various job training classes at Basic Training. I was surprised when Adam was selected for Military Police and sent to Camp Leonard Wood in Missouri. According to my plan for his life, he was to become a famous sports reporter on ESPN. But, I was overruled.

I couldn't contact him during the ten-week program, but I could follow the Army's website for details on their activities. I knew he was being trained in discipline, warrior tasks, and battle drills. I thought of all the little, green, plastic Army toys he played with as a boy. He was constantly on my mind, and I eagerly flew to Missouri for the graduation. I didn't recognize him at first and had to touch his face to make sure it was really him. He had lost 35 pounds in ten weeks. I momentary considered joining the military just for that reason, but quickly returned to my senses.

A few days later, he called with news that actually made me vomit and cry at the same time. He was to be stationed in South Korea as a military policeman. I resisted the urge to remind him that sports announcers didn't need to do that.

"I thought the recruiter said you would stay stateside," I gently said, wiping my mouth.

"He lied."

"How can I help?"

"Don't cry and puke the next time I call."

Adam was stationed at Camp Casey, forty miles north of Seoul, and the base was so isolated and dangerous it qualified for Hardship Duty pay. His job was to keep the peace, and that assignment included carrying a loaded gun and other weapons. My bartering with angels went into overdrive. "Name your price," I begged. "Just bring him home."

Military police had a difficult job because they were hated by the enemy and feared by their own soldiers. The average Korean was a foot shorter than Adam, so he was an easy target for the trigger-happy wackos over the border in North Korea. I gathered every religious symbol and talisman I could find, lit candles, mailed him funny gifts, and made daily promises to be good the rest of my life if he remained safe.

Mothers of soldiers and Marines share a fervent sisterhood, and I didn't choose to join the club but I was inducted anyway. I marked the days on a wall calendar. I found out later he was doing the same.

The only image I had of the military in South Korea was through the television series MASH. The show about characters in a Mobil Army Surgical Hospital parodied life and death during the Korean War. Ironically, the war lasted three years from 1950–1953, and the TV series was popular for twelve years, beginning in 1972.

"Can you pretend to be Corporal Klinger?" I asked during one of his rare telephone calls. "You know, the guy on MASH who always tried to gain a psychiatric discharge from the Army by wearing women's clothes? I could send you some dresses."

"No, Mom. I don't want any dresses. But could you send some real food? The grub over here tastes like animal dung covered with rotten seaweed."

"I'll send some cookies. I read in the online parent newsletter that I should pack them in popcorn so they won't break."

"Be sure to seal everything," he said. "Or the mice will get into the package. They're big as cats over here."

Only a few of the food packages I mailed were ever delivered. Either they were lost in the mail somewhere over the Pacific Ocean or they were confiscated by nefarious mail clerks. I decided to get serious about his Christmas present and went through the official Army gift website to order him a four-foot-tall Santa Claus figure. Santa arrived and brought a moment of cheer to Adam and his buddies stationed in a cold, bleak fortress north of Seoul during the holidays. When he finally returned to the mainland, he left Santa behind so another lonely soldier could take care of him.

Adam was proud to serve but after three years he was ready to leave Korea and the Army. Despite more promises of bigger bonuses and easy assignments in glorious locations around the world, he processed out of the military. When he returned, the spark in his eyes wasn't as dazzling, but it was still there and would return. I hugged him like a mother bear and then remembered I had to make good on all the promises I had made if he returned safely. I'm still working on those.

Due to his skills in the Army, he was hired immediately with the Ada County Sheriff's Department in Boise and chosen as a canine officer. I watched as he trained with the dog, and sometimes he wore padded suits and face masks to train with other dogs as they attacked him. There were times when I marveled at the transition he had made from a comical little boy to a competent, fearless professional. He loved the job. He worked ten-hour shifts dealing with criminals who called him a pig, car wrecks that killed children, dangerous traffic stops that needed his drug-sniffing dog, and complicated cases that required him to testify in court.

I recently watched a smug sports announcer express frustration about his job's long, stressful hours. I laughed.

"You'll never know, Buddy," I said. "You'll never know."

One day after work, Adam came to visit me. We shared stories and laughter, just like old times. Then he announced that he had met a woman named Danielle and she was special.

"Does she understand the job of a policeman?" I asked, knowing that the long, stressful hours could be difficult on a relationship and marriage.

"She works for the police department," he said. "She knows what we do."

"Well, that's good. But, most important, does she adore you and does she like to laugh?" I'm particular about those important traits in a potential mate.

"Yes." He smiled.

I could tell he was smitten. Obviously, he never intended for me to choose his career or his future wife. He did that all on his own, as he should. We met later and I agreed with Adam that she was a keeper. They married, settled in Boise, and raised spirited children while juggling jobs, a mortgage, bills, and activities. I watched and smiled. It seems as if I had been letting go for years, and it turned out to be okay. He was happy.

I gave him a tool box.

~

Balancing Midlife Without Falling Over

My friend Mary called and said she was coming over because the world was ending. I asked if she was bringing her survival gear and food storage supplies. She didn't laugh. Then she said, between sobs, that the marvelous guy she met through an online dating service turned out to be a con artist who lived overseas with several wives and assorted children. Because I had survived divorce, lost money to conniving men, and endured a host of personal and professional calamities, I had become the designated giver of advice for the forlorn and newly single.

"Come on over," I said. "I have wine and cookies."

Mary arrived with her miserable attitude of doom and gloom. I offered her the plate of cookies. She took four.

"How could I have been so stupid?" she said, dropping crumbs on her shirt as she talked around the bites of cookie. "We talked online for months. He said he was a wealthy doctor from New York and he traveled a lot doing operations for charities around the world."

I stifled a laugh. It was the ever-appealing traveling doctor story.

"He said he was flying here in his private jet to meet me," she said. "I bought a new outfit and canceled my trip to my 30th high school reunion."

"Oh, that's a tough one," I said. "You only get one 30th reunion."

"And then he called and said his plane broke down after carrying too many refugees to safety. He needed some money for a rare part to fix the plane so he could get here."

"No, you didn't send him any money," I said.

"Yes."

"How much?"

"More than $2,000." She burst into tears.

I gave her a tissue and waited for her to blow her nose and regain her composure. I knew it wouldn't be appropriate to call her a gullible loser. She already knew that.

We talked a bit and I encouraged her to learn from the mistake, become skeptical of everyone who started a relationship with her, and never send money to anyone unless she could buy me a new washing machine because mine was on its last spin cycle.

"I've been doing laundry for charity," I said. "So, any financial help would be appreciated."

"You're a pain in the ass," she said, and then she laughed.

"Keep laughing," I said. "That's how we survive."

We ended the conversation with a promise to stay in touch.

Middle-age women often asked me for advice about dating after age fifty. I tell them to note my three nonnegotiable nuggets of knowledge before baring their souls and body parts: keep a positive attitude, don't settle, and don't snore on the first date. Before they accept a date, shave their legs and exchange cargo pants for a sassy outfit, I suggest that they remember the three rules of engagement.

Keep a positive attitude. Maybe your date is apprehensive, too, and regrets that his high school physique graduated long ago and left the state. His priority might be to have an intelligent conversation with a witty, seasoned woman who dazzles him with her self-confidence and natural charm. There is about a ten percent chance that this fairy tale will come true, but don't give up.

Don't settle. I know a middle-aged woman so desperate for a relationship that she cavorted with a professional loser with no assets, no job potential, and without any socially redeeming value. He moved into her house, brought along his menagerie of dogs and snakes, and proceeded to deplete her refrigerator, bank account, and self-esteem. By the time she finally kicked out the dude, she was a ruined shell of a woman who sat alone in her backyard and talked to flies. Don't become that woman.

Don't snore on the first date. We all know first impressions are important, so that's why we check our teeth for broccoli, remove the toothpick, and change the salsa-stained shirt before meeting a new date. As for the snoring, I'm not suggesting that you hop into bed an hour after meeting. Wait at least a day or two. The snoring can result on the first date after you're so exhausted from a busy day that you fall asleep during a movie date and then make grotesque nasal sounds like a congested warthog with severe allergies. This unfortunate action can kill the romance before there is any chance of giggling down the hallway toward the playroom. If you think you might snore, stay awake. You'll thank me later.

Many middle-aged, unmarried women don't need to take a chance on dating and are happy with their single life. That's just fine. But for those who want to tiptoe back into the dating pool, feel free to jump in and make a big splash. After a few strokes, you might even feel confident enough to remove your life jacket and goggles.

As I approached my fifties, I retained my confident belief that nothing could ever make my panties bunch. I was battle-scarred but still standing. I decided to create a midlife survival plan and offer it to others, whether or not they are married, single, or none-of-the-above. Some women have been around the block enough times to know where to avoid the mud and dog poop or when to stop and smell the roses. Others, however, refuse to try a better path so they continue to trip over the same obstacles. And, then there is *that* group—the ones who stand in the street waiting for a free ride and then can't understand why they get hit by a bus.

My spirited and splendid journey through life has taught me that the secrets to survival can be condensed into a few easy paragraphs. It's short because so is life. Besides, we can't remember too many things at a time.

Use common sense. Spend less money than you make or you'll become a slave to debt which leads to misery, failure, and regret. Don't go on a zip line through the jungle if you have a bladder problem because there aren't any restrooms on those wobbly platforms. If you regularly eat an entire pecan pie with ice cream, you won't look good naked. See how it works? Our brains have the remarkable ability to make good or bad decisions and choices. My mature brain tells me to manage money, avoid zip lines, and not come within 10 miles of a pie.

Keep that pie image (and who wouldn't?) and acknowledge that input should balance output. If you consume more food than you need to survive, you should use enough energy to burn off the unnecessary calories. Get and stay healthy because life has a way of instantly whisking you from the high school prom to your 20-year reunion. And then it's just a few hours before you're sneaking into the store for reading glasses and incontinence supplies. Don't wait until you're older and lack the physical ability to skip with your grandchildren or chase your handsome hunk around the house, at different times of course.

Love to be in love. As the years go by, there is a profound sweetness in waking up with someone who accepts your wrinkles, thinning hair, and sagging body parts, and then says, "Good morning, gorgeous." Love your lover every day, from a passing wink to a sensual massage serenaded by Luther Vandross. A steady, exclusive relationship can turn a slow dance on the patio into a romantic encounter worthy of an evening in Paris. (Paris is always an adequate option.)

Bad things happen. No one gets a free pass on calamity. During your life, you probably will experience flat tires, funerals, diarrhea, lost love, fights with family, flatulence during a wedding, at least one broken bone, and the world's worst boss. So you get up again, adjust your armor and holler that you're ready for the next challenge. Looking back at the assorted chaos in my life, I realize there were far more splendid times than bad. And the truly amazing adventures happened after I initially failed or took a risk.

Attitude is everything. Positive, grateful people enjoy the best of life. By midlife, the laugh lines around their eyes reveal countless smiles through the miles, and their journey is one to emulate. Crabby, cynical worrywarts suck the energy from everyone they meet. Avoid them.

'Dear Abby' Pauline Phillips died a few years ago at the age of 94. Her advice columns appeared in 1,000 newspapers around the world. She wrote in her autobiography that her demanding job was not work because "It's only work if you'd rather be doing something else." I agree with her, and so my advice is to choose wisely, get healthy, love intensely, combat calamity, and be happy. Also, remember that life is short, so make it splendid.

Here's the perfect opportunity to talk about sex. And why not? It's not just for the youngsters with tight bodies and loose inhibitions. Some of us middle-aged grandmothers enjoy a regular dance between the sheets, and we don't care if that bothers anyone. Making love is so much better than leaning against the gyrating washing machine to stimulate sensual feelings of our former youth.

One of the many advantages of getting older is that we know what we like and don't like. And now we laugh when remembering those ten minutes of frantic fumbling in the back seat of a teenager's car after the high school game. At our age, we prefer Egyptian cotton sheets, soft jazz, and the luxury of foreplay. We're not only older but a lot wiser.

In their twenties, many men are so horny that a strong breeze could send their flag flying. This makes for an awkward situation when you're discussing your recent book club selection and your date is trying to hide the sudden tent in his pants. At fifty, it usually takes a longer time for men to get aroused, and that's just fine with the women.

Another reason to appreciate midlife canoodling is that at 25, most people are concerned about careers or finding and keeping a job. The stress can hamper performance in the bedroom, leading to frustration and more stress. After five decades, we've established our careers and know that there is life and love beyond the job. An embossed business card isn't necessary to prove our worth to a partner.

Most of us feel relieved that pregnancy is no longer possible. It's difficult for women over fifty to conceive. That's mainly because we don't want to get pregnant. We've raised our children and some of us have grandchildren, so there's no need to cry with joy or alarm over a pregnancy test. And, after a certain age, we no longer worry about getting a surprise period in the middle of a romantic vacation. The money I've saved by not buying feminine supplies now is used to stock my booze cabinet. This is a win-win situation.

We also know that children can cause "coitus interruptus." Those of us who had children in our twenties knew that passion was postponed for at least 18 years. If we got lucky and the kids were asleep, we could lock our bedroom door and try for a quickie. But as soon as we got going there came the predictable knock at the door from a little person who needed a drink of water or was puking on the carpet. By age fifty, the kids have moved out and on, so we can enjoy sex in the middle of the day and leave the bedroom door wide open. We also get to sleep naked, which further enhances any amorous opportunity.

One more comment about freedom to frolic after fifty: partners agree that what you see is what you get. I used to buy compression garments in multiple quantities and sizes and then stuff my aging body into the casing in order to look more attractive. As a result, I couldn't breathe and the constriction rearranged my internal organs until my liver was protruding over my cleavage. So I threw away the girdles, opened my robe, and presented my fifty-year-old body as a trophy. So far, my husband doesn't mind the prize. He's getting older, too, and I adore his laugh lines, silver hair, and experienced touch.

There are more reasons why life is better after age fifty, but most of us need to find out for ourselves how to navigate the changing rules and expectations. At the end of the day, we can relax, knowing we survived another day of trial and error without stabbing anyone. We refused to believe the guy online who promised to visit us in his private jet because, as Mary discovered, if the story sounded too good to be true, it probably was. Balancing midlife without falling over is a noble goal.

~

Blog Your Way to Fame and Shame

After my midlife divorce, I chose self-control to limit my caloric intake to only one carton of ice cream and one bottle of wine per day. This seemed a reasonable alternative to learning how to fold fitted sheets or organizing garage sales. Those activities would have been frustrating. In the midst of wallowing in my feelings of failure, my adult daughter Emily made a loving suggestion.

"It's time to get off your butt, Mom," she said. "You should write a blog."

"What's a blog?" I asked. "Does it require thought and energy?"

"It's just what you need," she said. "You love to write, and I'll show you how to set up a website. Let's see if we can get your domain name."

It all sounded like a lot of thought and energy, but I decided to try. I didn't want Emily to think her mother was a washed up pile of junk. She had believed I was a loser when she was a teenager, but then all the teenagers thought all the moms were losers, and we were past that. She really cared about me and wanted me to join the family again. She may have saved me.

With a few quick strokes on my computer keyboard, my daughter secured my domain name. Then she showed me how to build a website, format an article in a Word document, and insert it as a blog on my site. I was inspired to continue, and over the next few years published more than 500 posts on my blog and on other social media platforms. The experience energized my life, and I reduced the amount of ice cream and wine. Somewhat.

Many midlife women reinvent themselves by creating and writing a blog. It keeps our brains active so we don't fill the empty nest with bubble bath and take a 10-year soak. By writing, we can tell our stories and gain respect among our peers. Or, we can tell our stories and humiliate ourselves throughout the world. I have accomplished both goals.

The term blog is a combination of the words web log, and I started writing a blog in my fifties. I encourage women over age fifty to write a blog, not for fame but to activate their brains and create stories others will enjoy reading. The kids were grown and had moved out, I had left a full-time corporate job, and I had time to write. A blog is the perfect hobby because anyone can write and publish it at any time from home. Blogs can be personal, just to share with selected family and friends, or they can be public and published on the Internet for all the world to read.

More than 200 million blogs are active on various platforms, and a new blog is started every second of every hour. But you need to do something with that extra 30 minutes a day. Start writing, and discover where your muse leads. You could write about family, travel, humor, politics, recipes, the empty nest, or inspirational themes. Your experiences matter, especially if you can write and tell a story.

After establishing a blog, apply to several online sites that will accept your work. I prefer *The Huffington Post, BlogHer, Project Eve, Humor Outcasts,* and *Midlife Boulevard.* Find your tribe and connect with others who share your passion. It's like sitting around the table sharing anecdotes with best friends you'll never meet. Remember that you have the potential to impact, humor, irritate, and enlighten audiences around the world.

Here's a key fact you already knew: Farts are hilarious. I learned this interesting truth after writing a silly 600-word essay that appeared on *The Huffington Post Comedy* page. The post titled "Don't Fart During an MRI" went viral with more than 800-thousand likes on social media, and it was translated into six different languages from around the world. I received e-mails from readers in other countries thanking me for my story, and it followed me everywhere. My viral blog post turned me into the butt of too many jokes.

I'm a bit perplexed by the notoriety because I've been writing professionally for forty years and it took a fart to gain me the largest audience. I should have skipped my stressful jobs in corporate communications, let her rip, and written as a 12-year-old boy.

Don't Fart During an MRI

I share this true but pathetic story to commiserate with other tortured souls who relentlessly endure and survive extreme humiliation. My experience will be difficult to surpass: I farted inside an MRI machine.

In medical terms, I had torn the meniscus cartilage that acts as a shock absorber between my shinbone and thighbone. In middle-age woman terms, two demons from hell invaded my body and lit fires in my knee and then danced around poking the raw nerves with electric forks. The pain was beyond intense, and the accident severely damaged my body so I couldn't stand, walk, or even crawl to the wine bar.

Five drug-induced days later, I finally saw an orthopedic surgeon. He manipulated my knee until tears streamed down my cheeks and I threatened to tear off his arms. It should have been obvious that I was injured by the way I was ripping off chunks from the sides of the examination table. I silently vowed to add him as a nasty character in my next short story. Finally, some lovely angel gave me legal narcotics. Soon my ravaged leg was a big, bandaged joke, and I laughed and laughed.

A few days later I experienced the MRI, a magnetic resonance imaging procedure that produces images of damaged ligaments and joints. A handsome young technician helped me into the tube of terror and strapped down my leg. I nervously remarked that a first name usually was required before I allowed anyone to tie me in a bed. He didn't laugh but ordered me to hold still for 45 minutes.

So there I was, in pain, suffering from claustrophobia, moving on a conveyor belt into the white torture chamber, and I didn't have a clue how to remain motionless. And, to complete the distress, my only audience wasn't amused by my jokes.

After about 20 minutes, I started to get anxious. I was tied down in a tunnel and could only hear strange beeping noises and grinding sounds. For all I knew, they were deciding which body parts to extract and sell on the black market. Then a queasy feeling predicted a pending passing of gas. I bit my tongue, pinched my side, and tried to focus on a pastoral scene in a green meadow beside a babbling brook. I could hear my mother's advice:

"Squeeze the dime." I fidgeted.

"Please hold still," came a voice from outside the shaft of shame.

I watched as the lights and numbers revealed how much time remained. Three minutes. I could do it! No! My body betrayed me at the one-minute mark. I was trapped and helpless so my nervous body did what it does best: it farted. I released gas with the intensity and conviction of a team of sumo wrestlers after a chili-eating contest. And the confined space caused the sound to be amplified as if a dozen foghorns had simultaneously activated. I didn't know whether to cry, giggle, or call my son and brag.

"Well now, I think we have enough images," the handsome technician said, suppressing a laugh.

The magic bed moved backwards into freedom, bringing along the putrid stench of decay. I was mortified as my imaginary meadow became a ravaged pasture full of rotting manure. What in the hell had I eaten? I avoided eye contact with the timid technician and hobbled back to the dressing room. Once again, I accepted my fate of being the perpetual, reluctant clown, the oddball, the one who farts during a complicated medical procedure.

If I ever need another MRI, I'll request a facility in Texas. Everyone farts there.

(I don't need any complaints from people in Texas. I wrote Texas because Massachusetts was too difficult to spell.)

I continued to blog about my injury and exploit the chances of having another viral blog. After more than 100 posts on *The Huffington Post*, several essays received hundreds of responses, but none ever permeated the rarified air of going viral. I made one last attempt to write about my knee injury. Here is that blog post.

Hallucinating with Storybook Friends

As an adult, I often experience profound public humiliation with a daunting magnitude that would send most people screaming into the forest, never to return. I've learned to accept the fact that I probably would have a sudden attack of explosive diarrhea and projectile vomiting while riding on a crowded bus without a potty. I'll accidentally belch during a sensuous massage, stab myself cutting fruit, or sprout broccoli and glitter in my teeth while giving a motivational speech. I've become a self-contained comedy and calamity routine, and I have the stitches, scars, crutches, plaster casts, and eye patches to prove it.

One wretched story began with hallucinations with storybook friends and digressed straight to a tragedy of epic proportions. I recently fell during a rigorous exercise movement called the "speed skater." I was in a class with tight-bodied women half my age, and I wanted to show I could leap and touch the ground with the ease of a delicate ballerina. Reality can be cruel. I wasn't young, never could ice skate, and possessed the grace of a lumbering rhinoceros. I completed a series of exhausting movements and then crashed with a sound that moved the local geological seismograph.

I experienced a knee injury so painful that I sobbed until tears and snot covered my face. Studley, my saintly husband, insisted on taking me to the hospital. For once, I ignored my mother's admonition to wear clean underwear in case I was in an accident. For years, I dutifully obeyed for fear that during an emergency the medical personnel would rush to my rescue but suddenly stop tending my injuries.

I imagined the EMT muttering in disgust, "Look Bob, this one isn't wearing clean underwear. Let 'er bleed to death!"

After x-rays confirmed a cracked bone and a torn meniscus, a doctor who appeared to be twelve years old prescribed an assortment of painkilling medicines. I wanted to adopt him because the wonder drugs were magnificent.

I had been proud of my ability to avoid illegal drugs, even while growing up during the sixties and seventies, but after experiencing the magical pills I wondered if my pious virtue and self-discipline had been overrated. As my husband drove us home from the hospital, I was enjoying my own private trip.

I noticed a large white rabbit sitting in the back seat and recognized him as one of the characters in the book *Alice's Adventures in Wonderland,* a childhood favorite.

"Hi, White Rabbit!" I said and waved. Studley kept driving.

Then I looked out the window and saw the Cheshire Cat grinning in the night sky. His head turned all the way around and I laughed with delight.

"Look! The cat is winking at me!" Studley kept driving.

We arrived home and my patient, strong husband wrestled my incapacitated body out of the car, into the house, and onto the bed. By then, there was an entire damn tea party floating around the room. Alice looked at me with a sigh of boredom and begged me to get up and play. The Dormouse scolded Alice for being bossy so the Mad Hatter and the White Rabbit pushed his head into the teapot. I laughed and laughed.

I noticed the Caterpillar sitting on a pillow smoking a hookah. He offered me a toke but I told him I'd never inhaled. That statement caused everyone at the party to spit out their tea, and I felt silly. Just then the Queen of Hearts ran into the bedroom waving a big ax.

"Off with her head!" she screamed.

I hollered for help, and the beleaguered man came running so fast he almost spilled his gin and tonic.

"What's the matter?" he asked. "Do you need more pain pills?"

"Yes, yes," I gasped. "And paint the white roses red so the queen won't cut off my head!"

He patiently read the instructions on the pill bottle and considered having a few but decided I needed them more.

"You need to wait two more hours," he said.

I clenched my fists and snarled. Studley feared for his life.

"I need another pill," I growled with the intensity of the possessed girl in *The Exorcist.*

By then Studley was reminiscing about his single life, just a short five years ago. Nothing had prepared him for life with a writer whose imagination was prone to hallucinations, even while sober. The pain meds introduced a whole new level of crazy.

He gulped his gin and bravely offered three ibuprofen tablets.

"Take these," he suggested. "They'll help until it's time for the hydrocodone. Remember, this prescription is a narcotic related to opium."

"But look at the Caterpillar," I wailed. "He's smoking a hookah on your pillow!"

Studley nodded and left to fix another cocktail. That's when a pink flamingo peeked from underneath the sheet. He whispered that he needed to hide because Alice wanted to use him as a croquet mallet. I promised and pulled up the sheet.

I vaguely remember falling down a hole lined with red roses. *The queen should be happy with that,* I thought. Then everything went black. But I know that the flamingo stayed underneath the sheet because I could hear him snoring and moaning all night. Or was that me?

Another blog was selected as a "Voices of the Year" winner in the annual competition sponsored by BlogHer.com. I traveled to New York City to participate in the awards ceremony and shared the stage with other winners who wrote dynamic pieces about women's rights, survival, and motivation. Again, I was comic relief because I wrote about my mother's missing casket. Here's the winning post.

My Mother's Body Got Lost

I was trying to plan my mother's funeral, but we had a problem. We couldn't find her.

My mother passed away after a long illness. I had all the funeral arrangements planned months in advance, so I was prepared when the inevitable happened. After she died, I contacted the proper authorities to transport her body 100 miles to her hometown of Wendell, Idaho for the funeral and burial. Some things don't always go as planned. Two days later, we knew that the body was gone from her assisted living facility but it was not in Wendell. This was a cause for concern.

During the past few years, my mother has been lost in dementia. Even after moving her to a secure nursing home in Boise, there were times when I visited and couldn't find her. The staff and I would search the facility and find her in someone else's room and the two residents would be talking about their old times that never happened. No harm was done, and we gently, lovingly participated in their storytelling. But, I always knew she was somewhere inside the building.

After the initial shock that my mother's body was really missing, I called the funeral home in Wendell and they hadn't received the body. How do you lose a casket? I thought I had completed all the necessary arrangements, but I wasn't familiar with the procedures for this dilemma. I used my inside voice and calmly requested that somebody do something. I called back an hour later and needed to employ my outside, aggressive tone. This last resort has been known to get immediate results and leave people trembling. I'm not proud of this trait, but it works.

At last, I received a call from Wendell that they had found her body still in Boise and the transportation was being arranged. A few hours later, I received a call that said she was near Bliss, a tiny village along the route.

"Of course she is," I responded.

Planning a funeral is similar to planning a wedding. Family and friends come together, some cry, music plays, and people wave goodbye. Except, at a funeral, the goodbye lasts a long time. This last momentary interruption is my mother's way of telling me I'm not in charge of everything. I hope she had a nice weekend and enjoyed having the last word. Somewhere, my parents were laughing.

Besides gaining readers and receiving recognition, many bloggers monetize their writing and receive additional perks and rewards. Some writers are opposed to writing for free, and I don't blame them. It's nice to get paid for our work, and "exposure" won't pay the bills. But, sometimes a silly blog submitted on a prominent site can result in unexpected income.

A few months after my viral farting post, I began to receive e-mails from around the world and only can conclude that people in Korea like fart stories. E-mails came from MRI technicians requesting permission to hang a copy of the article in the waiting room where patients were waiting for an MRI. Other requests came for permission to reprint in various medical, midlife, and humor magazines and websites. One website published without permission and omitted my name. I shamed them on social media.

My posts on *The Huffington Post* were not compensated, but my profile is on every post and it includes a link to my website, displays the covers of my two latest books, and adds links for how to purchase the books online. The sales of those books increased dramatically after the fart blog. I recently received payment for paperbacks and e-books sold since the blog was published, and the income was enough to pay off all my credit cards. I could truthfully say that a fart helped pay my bills.

The e-book of *Midlife Cabernet* rose to #1 in sales in the humor category and #3 in the top 100 books sold in all categories.

The other value to blogging is that it uses my brain. It's difficult for me to sit down and write 3,000 words for my next book, but a 500-word blog takes an hour or two. I enjoy creating a brief message that I hope is witty or at least enlightening. I finally learned how to add photographs and publish a cohesive blog on my website. It takes a few more minutes to post the blog to various sites, then I can relax and eat cookies and drink a celebratory glass of wine.

Some writers will scoff at the lack of literary value of my humorous blogs, and others will negatively judge my willingness to forfeit my professional reputation by capitalizing on a story for the 10-year-old boys within us. They have every right to hunker down and sweat over crafting the perfect sentence. (Is there one?) I, too, can write serious prose and I'm working on a memoir that is not humorous. But for now, I'll just walk to the bank, farting all the way.

Another way to obtain complimentary products and services is to agree to write about the company. I wrote a blog about my free plastic surgery procedure.

Searching for Cheekbones

I never intended to have hyaluronic acid gel injected into my face, but the physician said he could smooth my nasolabial folds. I love it when a guy talks dirty to me.

"How do you know they need improvement?" I cooed.

"Those are your laugh lines around your mouth," he answered. "You must laugh a lot."

Well, yes I do. But I've earned every line on my face and I was hesitant to try to cover up the damage from six decades of living out loud. And the procedure involved needles. I hate needles.

At the recent Bloggers at Midlife Conference in Las Vegas, Nevada, the trade show featured demonstrations of a gel that could be injected to contour faces. A few women were chosen for the injections, and I obviously appeared to be the perfect "before" candidate. A team of goddess-faced professionals consulted me before showing the tray of syringes and gave me some literature to read.

The procedure implanted hyaluronic acid gel below the surface of the skin to correct moderate facial wrinkles and to give definition to shapeless cheeks and correct age-related midface contour deficiencies in patients over the age of 21. Lucky for me, I was over 21 and had the round face of Charlie Brown. The demonstration came at no cost, so I decided why not? Like a brave, wrinkled soldier, I assumed the position on the table.

"As long as we're here, could you perform liposuction on my entire body?" I asked.

"We don't have enough time or big enough equipment," he answered. What a joker.

The procedure took about 15 minutes. He injected the gel into the lines around my mouth, muttering that he was a great sculptor and I was his work of art. I felt more like a massive lump of pottery clay.

Then he injected the solution along my cheeks. I've been blessed with a round balloon face, so I've never seen my cheekbones. I assumed they were in there somewhere. After the injections, I could immediately see the definition on my face. A few more glasses of wine and I would look like Sophia Loren.

A few hours after the injections, I could see that my marionette puppet mouth was less hinged. I could pass for a glamorous fifty-year-old. After age 60, it's all relative.

I appreciate the complimentary lift, and it's interesting to see the slight contours in my face. I've read that some women curtail their laughter so they won't develop laugh lines. That's a sacrifice I'm not willing to make. For now, I'll keep laughing and see if the lines return. We'll see how interesting my nasolabial folds can become.

Find a niche, seek out others, and publish your essays. Read other blogs to emulate their style. Attend blogging conventions and listen to online podcasts. Who knows? Someday you may be famous in Australia for farting! It's a reward that lingers and you can take it anywhere.

~

My Fish Won't Hump Your Leg

"Why is it masturbating on my white pants?" I asked, trying to remain calm.

"He's just so friendly," my laughing hostess proclaimed, as if expecting me to enjoy the animal's affection.

We had arrived at our host's lovely home and exchanged pleasantries as I offered my baked won-ton appetizers. Then the dog attacked. The pony-sized labradoodle bounded into the room and feverishly started to hump my leg with the passion of a sailor on shore leave.

She retrieved the dog and nuzzled its face. That's when I knew it would be a long evening. I walked briskly toward the wine bar, wary of sudden attacks from the horny hound. Once again, grapes would get me through the ordeal.

I belong to that rare and happy group of people who don't have indoor pets. Every day my friends on social media post photos and videos of cats and dogs, and I quickly scroll past these visions because I know that the dog licked its genitals before it licked that sweet baby's face. And unless the child has been raised and suckled by wolves in the forest, the baby doesn't need to sleep with an animal. At the risk of being pelted with stale dog biscuits and bitten by animal rights activists, I politely request that pet lovers accept the fact that some of us prefer not to live with hairballs, poop behind the couch, and animal hair in our food.

One day I saw my pet-loving friend Sue prancing through a parking lot. She waved me to come over.

"Look at my new baby," she said as she proudly presented a fancy carrier. "Isn't he adorable?"

I peeked inside to see a small ball of fur with two eyes and a tongue. Adorable? Not to me. But, I liked Sue so tried to appreciate her passion for pets.

"That's a cute little dog," I said, sticking to the facts.

"He's such a good boy," Sue gushed. Really, pet owners need to acquire new descriptions. I didn't know or care if he was a good boy.

"Why are you carrying him in a purse?" I asked.

"This is the latest travel item for pets. We can take him on an airplane in this."

"That's great," I said. "I find it so comfortable to travel for hours in a cramped seat next to an animal in a cage."

"Don't be silly. Some people love their pets and take them everywhere."

"I loved my kids, but I always had to buy them their own seat on the plane. The airline wouldn't allow me to pack them in a purse."

Another time, I was playing with my children in a local park. Friends came over with their dogs on leashes. While we chatted, my kids went nuts petting the dogs. Another friend appeared, also with a leashed dog. The dogs became animated and began to sniff each other's butts.

"They're just getting to know each other," one owner said, laughing.

"I prefer a handshake," I answered.

One of the dogs squatted and dropped a pile in the grass. My friend kept talking to me, removed a plastic baggie from her pocket, picked up the steaming mound of poop, closed the bag, and never missed a word of conversation. I choose not to do that activity, and will live a good life without ever snatching dog poop in a baggie.

I grew up on a farm surrounded by fields and pens full of cattle, horses, pigs, a few cats, and a dog. None of these animals lived inside our house. The dog provided security by barking at dangerous squirrels and by herding cattle. The cats worked daily as mousers in the barn. Not one of them wore a sweater vest or needed a therapist. We all knew our roles down on the farm, and life was grand.

Pet-less people never have dead mice delivered to their doorstep by a warrior cat or hear the blood-curdling scream of cats in heat. They don't need to worry about getting a kennel when they travel, and they save money by not buying pet food or dealing with expensive veterinarian bills. Americans spend more than $56 billion annually on pets. We could fix some roads, supply new books to the schools, and build animal sanctuaries with that money.

Caveat: I respect those who need indoor animals for comfort and companionship. And, I'm a firm supporter of service dogs and police canine units. These animals earn their keep and provide an important duty.

I have the perfect pets: fish. My outside pond is full of goldfish and koi. They are beautiful, don't demand anything, and don't chew my furniture. Best of all, in the winter they hibernate in the rocks and don't need anything. A working replica of the famous statue Mannekin Pis, a bronze sculpture in Brussels that depicts a naked little boy urinating into a fountain, stands at the edge and helps water the pond. I'm not sure what statement the statue is declaring, but it makes me smile.

I intend to enjoy my patio for many years and watch my goldfish and koi swim around. Guests are welcome to visit—without any pets—sip a glass of wine, and offer a toast to my fish. I promise they won't hump any legs.

I remember when my children were young and begged me to have a pet.

"But, Mom," they wailed. "Every kid has a dog. Why don't we?"

"Because I said so," I offered, knowing that line had never worked before. I suspected they would grow up permanently scarred, traumatized with being deprived, and threaten to write a tell-all book about me. I wasn't deterred, despite their begging.

"You remember those shoes you needed for school?" I said, opting for the well-used guilt tactic of parenting. "And that vacation last summer? Well, your dad and I both work full-time to make money to pay for those things and we don't have one extra minute to add a pet to our schedule of jobs, kids, meals, shopping, and attempting to keep the clutter low enough to open the door."

"But MOOOOOMMMM," my son Adam cried, making the word stretch to ten syllables. "I promise to take care of a puppy."

I stared at him. He cocked his head in the adorable way that usually meant he could have anything he wanted for the rest of his life and I would die trying to fulfill his every wish. That still didn't work. There was no way in hell I was going to take an additional 15 minutes out of my five hours of sleep to clean up poop, hairballs, or animal hair. That wasn't going to happen.

My children knew how to manipulate my emotions, mainly because they were so stinking cute. My son continued to plead for a puppy but all I could imagine was a scenario where I was hurrying downstairs to get the kids fed and to school but slipping in puppy pee on the floor. Believe it or not, some humans do not like puppies. I'm unfit for any commercial that includes pets. Children are just fine, however, and I do enjoy watching the horses on the Budweiser beer commercials.

One day Adam tried the bouquet of flowers bribe which had worked when he wanted the Dallas Cowboys football helmet, limited edition. I had agreed to the helmet for his birthday because helmets don't need to be fed and walked. For his updated appeal, he appeared with a chubby fistful of colorful roses he had swiped from the neighbor's flowerbed.

"Here, Mommy," he said. My named changed from Mom to Mommy depending upon the motivation and desired result. "Here are some flowers because you are so nice and pretty."

"They're so beautiful," I gushed, reaching for a vase. "Thank you so much."

He stood proudly and watched as I filled the vase with water and arranged the roses. I waited for the plea.

"Have you thought anymore about us having a puppy?" His voice was so sweet, and he included the head tilt. "My friend Jason said his dog is a watch dog and protects the family in case there is danger outside."

I was impressed with his improved debating skills. This kid had a future in sales and marketing.

"Oh, Sweetie," I answered. "I don't know if we're ready for a dog. How about a compromise? If you want a pet, we'll get a hamster first and see how the family can adjust."

"A hamster isn't a dog."

"I know. But, we'll get a cute cage with a fun exercise wheel. If you can take care of the hamster, feed it, clean the cage, and not lose it under my bed, then we can consider getting other pets."

He studied the situation, hands on hips. I could tell he was thinking that the compromise might be worth the trouble if it meant getting a dog.

"Okay," he said. "But I get to name it and keep it in my room."

"Deal."

The following weekend, we visited the pet store and purchased the hamster and all the necessary supplies. Adam loved it and named it Benny. I thought it looked like a fat rat.

For the next few weeks, Adam diligently cleaned the cage, added fresh water and food, and played with Benny. I was surprised that he took pride in his responsibility to care for the pet. I decided to give the plan another month. Three weeks later, I passed his room and the stench made my eyes water. I bravely opened the door and was greeted with the aroma of an abundant collection of hamster feces. For such a little creature, he sure could produce a mess of foul-smelling poop.

I grabbed the cage, took it outside, slid open the trap door on the bottom of the cage, and emptied all the contents into the garbage can. The confused hamster sought shelter in his wheel. Then I filled the cage with clean bedding, added some food and water, and drove it to the local child care center with all the necessary supplies. I knew the owner and she was delighted to have a free pet for the kids to enjoy. It took another four weeks for my children to notice that Benny was gone. I proved my point.

My children now have homes of their own, and they each have an indoor dog. That's fine with me. We've worked out a compromise where I tolerate their love of pets and they tolerate my love of my fish. Maybe someday I'll bring my son's children some fish in a converted Dallas Cowboys football helmet. I'll throw in pom-poms for free.

~

Still Laughing in the Empty Nest

The Midlife Happy Hour Club met to celebrate the college graduation of Linda's daughter. Our conversation turned to the joys and struggles of parenthood. We had, by some unknown factor of luck, raised our children without causing too much permanent damage to them or to ourselves. We felt entitled to offer our esteemed parenting advice for the rest of the world from the security of our table at Twigs Bar. Such advice was meant to be taken with a grain of salt, preferably licked from the rims of our margarita glasses.

"I think parents of young children are too fragile and overly worried about providing the perfect nurturing environment for their little darlings," I said. "I've been embarrassing my children for more than thirty years, and now they are happy adults with loving spouses, adorable children, and rewarding careers. Obviously, my strategy worked."

"I agree," Nancy said as she sipped her Lemon Drop martini. "Throughout my kids' childhood, I didn't worry about harming their delicate self-esteem. Nor did I hover over their every action, schedule daily enrichment activities, make them eat kale, or ensure their socks matched."

"I intentionally created chaos and commotion just to motivate them to find peace and create order in their lives," I replied, tasting the salt on the edge of my margarita. "I'm altruistic like that."

We worried that children were more pampered than a child pharaoh, and their timid parents could become marooned in a horrifying, never-ending reality show if they didn't stop appeasing and indulging their tiny terrors. To toughen kids for real life, we devised a list of outrageous activities that bewildered parents should do to challenge their children's self-confidence and encourage self-reliance. Our ridiculous suggestions became bolder with each sip of our cocktails. Kitty, the most organized, took out pen and paper to write the list as we made up the rules. We continued to grin at our own self-imposed award for creating such great humor.

"Criticize their artwork," said Jennifer. "If your first-grader comes home with a hand-drawn picture, be sure to say that the tree looks like a spider and the sun should be more round. Then throw it away. Maybe she'll try harder."

"Show favoritism," Debby said. "If the older child has an attractive project, be sure to tape it to the refrigerator for months and often mention the talent to the younger one. Give the older child extra dessert."

"Exhibit lazy behavior," was Linda's contribution. "Stay in bed on Saturday morning and tell them to make their own damn pancakes. This is how children learn responsibility and cooking skills."

Kitty's suggestion came next. "Take your own time-out. If the children are throwing a fit, sit on the floor and chant in a foreign language for several minutes. They'll be too traumatized to make noise."

"Condemn their friends," Nancy said. "Be sure to mock their friends' silly habits. And when your teenager has a basement full of rowdy kids, walk in wearing a clown nose, belch loudly, and walk out. This instills a fear in your child that never goes away."

We laughed at our profound display of astute knowledge about all things relating to parenthood. We ordered another round and continued with our nontraditional instructional manual.

"Cry when you meet your child's first date. Sob into a towel, run into your room, and slam the door. This action will test their patience, strengthen their loyalty to each other, and promote tolerance."

"Threaten them, if necessary. If your high school senior won't write thank you notes for graduation presents, threaten to publish an announcement on social media that your child is too lazy and ungrateful to appreciate gifts now or in the future."

"Bribery works. That hellhole of a bedroom won't get clean on its own. Hide a $10 bill somewhere in the room and tell them to tidy and organize everything to find it. Substitute a $20 bill for particularly egregious cases that harbor toxic diseases. If they demand more money, tell them to move out and find an apartment."

"Remember that children can sense an easy target. If mommy and daddy are too weak and delicate to assume their strong but loving roles as parents, the kids will rule the house before the youngest is out of diapers and could stay in diapers for ten years. Parents can reverse this pending disaster by starting now to embarrass their children on a regular basis so the kids find the courage to grow up, move out, and prove themselves."

A group of younger women noticed our brash behavior and wandered over to discover what was so funny. We invited them to join us and explained that we were compiling tongue-in-cheek advice to an imaginary group of young women seeking advice on how to juggle family, job, home, community, and themselves. We wanted to tell them the answers don't come until they reach midlife when they finally realize they can't control everything. The motivated overachievers in the thirty-year-old crowd should learn to ease off the quest for perfection, or they will implode and probably become fifty-year-old poets singing torch songs for tips in a dark lounge across the border.

"You're right," said a woman in the new group. "I often feel like a clown in a circus. I'm spinning a dozen flaming torches while peddling a unicycle on a high wire as the out-of-tune calliope wheezes a medley of manic music."

"The clown has an easier reality because her show ends at 10:00 p.m.," said another woman. "We still have two loads of laundry, a sink full of dirty dishes, The Spawn needs cupcakes for school in the morning, and Romeo wants to score tonight."

I reminded them that all the dishes and laundry would never be done until they were well into their fifties, and way too soon The Spawn will have a tart of his own and won't need their culinary skills. That left Romeo. I said to turn off the lights (to add romance and hide the dust bunnies,) don something flimsy, and go for it while they're still awake. At least do it to relieve tension.

My friends and I were working mothers back in the olden days when women were supposed to stay home, wear pearls with aprons, and make casseroles that included canned soup and frozen peas. I should have added crescent rolls but I could never get those damn cans to pop at the seams. They always exploded onto the ceiling, so I just left the dough to hang and harden in mysterious clumps and called it art.

My kids would be positively giddy if I cooked the pasta first before serving their favorite macaroni and cheese dinner. But, I usually didn't have time to boil water so I encouraged them to chew slowly and enjoy all the roughage. That was back during the early 1980s, before computers, cell phones, and Oprah. I had to find enlightenment and empowerment on my own while fighting the urge to run away and join the circus.

During the work week, we existed on five hours of sleep, fed the kids, took them to child care, worked nine hours, retrieved the little darlings, concocted something edible for dinner, gave them baths, read stories, and tucked them into bed. Then we did the housework while some clueless zealot chortled on television about bringing home the bacon, frying it in a pan, and then pleasing my man. Hell, in reality I wanted to throw some bologna in the microwave, serve it on paper plates, snuggle into my worn t-shirt, and read a book without pictures.

I want young mothers to know that the merry-go-round eventually stops and you can get off, maybe with the help of a sturdy cane. Age brings a certain freedom and wisdom that is elusive when you're under age 40. My kids now are creating their own personal circuses at home, and I enjoy grabbing some popcorn, taking my place in the bleachers, and cheering from the sidelines. And, by now I don't have to clean up after the elephants.

"Do you remain close to your grown children?" a woman asked. "Do they want your advice?"

"It's still tempting to give advice but only when asked," I said. "My adult daughter dyed her hair purple as mine turned gray. She's proud of her colorful hair and elaborate tattoos because they accent her independent style. She sets her own schedule and teaches physical and mental health to her loyal clients through her private fitness and wellness studio. I have thin hair and gnarly age spots, and I tell jokes until people snort beer from their noses. Though we have varied techniques of pleasing our intended audiences, we guarantee customer satisfaction and life isn't boring."

"My daughter and I have shared the peaks and valleys of life with more volatility than a game of fetch with a junkyard dog," said Debby. "At least we've passed the wretched teenage years when she would wail, 'Stop looking at me!'"

"What about getting older?" a young woman asked. "Do you worry what will happen if you can't take care of yourself?"

I offered an honest answer. "My daughter is my designated Power of Attorney over health care and she knows I wouldn't want to live without independence. In fact, she said not to worry because if I'm ever on life support, she'll pull the plug. She really does love me."

"Do you miss your children after they're gone?"

"Of course I do," I said. "My son and I used to laugh and tell such fabulous stories. Sometimes I throw some wet towels on the floor and scatter plates of food around the house just to remember what it was like when we lived together."

The young women laughed and thanked us for the conversation. We ended our impromptu social hour by exchanging encouragement and laughter. They needed to hurry home to tackle a dozen chores. We had to go home and find some comfortable sweatpants. Growing older does have its rewards.

~

Midlife Crisis of Confidence

One day around my 45th birthday, I noticed that my body was missing and had been replaced by a strange person I barely recognized. The boobs were sprawling on my lap but the eyesight was too poor to notice. The only benefit was that the monthly periods had stopped. Was this a midlife crisis or just a crisis in confidence? My other friends noticed similar physical and mental incidents with their own bodies and were in a quandary whether to blissfully accept the changes or adopt the anti-aging war cry.

"I swear," muttered Linda. "It's a good thing I have a keen sense of humor to accept what is happening to my body. My hair is so thin my scalp shines in the dark but there is a patch of growth thick as a muskrat on my chin and toes."

"Damnit, go ahead and swear," I said. "My body has been abducted and replaced with a ball of bread dough that can't be punched down. And the boobs! Gravity has relocated my once-perky breasts down near my knees. It's only a matter of time before I'm pushing them in a cart."

Studley, my patient and wise husband, overheard the conversation and offered his objective analysis of gravity.

"Did you know that when you step on a scale, it reads how much gravity is acting on your body?"

We stared at him with a look that told him to leave the room or suffer bodily harm.

"Bless your heart," Linda said.

"Apparently, I attract a great amount of gravity," I said, winking at Studley as he left the room. "That's more proof that gravity is not my friend because I fall down all the time. When I attempt to balance on one foot in yoga class, my tree pose topples to the ground. The result is not conducive to peaceful meditation when I was rolling around moaning and groaning."

I didn't pay attention to the sagging boobs issue until I noticed in photographs that my youthful hourglass shape had settled comfortably into a rotund grandfather clock. Instead of retaining my splendid, 20-something physique, I was regressing to the toddler stage with thin hair, pudgy belly, clumsy walk, and the need for a nap. This realization made me crave a bottle; one that wasn't full of milk.

A scholarly research of medical facts taught me that breasts naturally sag because the ligaments break down as the collagen and elastin lose the will to get up in the morning. I found a nastier explanation that age causes dense glandular tissue to be replaced by fat that is more likely to droop. Ultimately, two of my best assets had become fat-filled tittie tubes.

In defiance, I purchased industrial-strength bras with pulley-system straps that could ratchet the migrating mammary glands off my belt. However, this caused my ta-tas to resemble military missiles ready to launch and clothes to drape like a cheap holiday cloth over a sturdy buffet table.

Due to my matronly profile, I could set a book and a full wineglass on my uplifted chest. So I did.

Further research explained that physical exercise won't redeem the wayward jugs. Push-ups couldn't reduce the droop because breasts are made of fat not muscle, so I decided *not* to attempt 100 push-ups every morning. Other causes included smoking, which I've never done, and sun bathing, which I've never done in the nude, in compliance with obscenity laws. High-fat diets can contribute to sagging boobs, but then what's left of life to enjoy? One cannot live by wine alone! Would this bosom bounce back to where it belonged if I didn't butter my corn or drown my warm berry pie with ice cream? I think not!

A friend who specializes in homeopathic treatments brought me a list of the top ten top home remedies for firming sagging breasts.

"Try these suggestions," she murmured gently as organic bean sprouts appeared from her naturally-curly hair and a mist of lavender puffed from her youthful pores like glitter in a unicorn's breath.

I dropped my nachos and cocked my salon-treated mess of a haircut. "Let me get this off my chest," I said. "My rack has fallen and can't get up. Your potions and lotions won't help."

"Your negative energy is blocking your healing chakra," she said, her voice matching the perfect pitch of a dove's coo. "Meditate on lifting your soul so the spirit realm can help revitalize whatever brings you down." She turned to go and seemed to vanish in a cloud of non-allergenic fairy dust.

I opened a beverage and practiced positive thoughts as I sipped and read her list. One technique involved massaging olive oil gently over the breasts for 15 minutes to increase blood flow and stimulate cell repair. Studley dutifully volunteered to administer this remedy as often as necessary. He wasn't so excited about the next suggestion to apply a paste of pureed cucumber and egg yolk because he preferred his salad on a plate. I determined the list was a bust, so I unhooked the constrictions and flung the bindings to the far corner.

"Let them be free!" I shouted from the depths of my bosom.

Then I ran naked to the hot tub, mimicking Kathy Bates in the Jacuzzi scene from the movie *About Schmidt.* Incidentally, that scene was voted by a men's magazine as the "Most Ball Clenching Movie Moment of All Time." Not even Jack Nicholson could keep a straight face. As the warm water caused my girls to float upward, I shook my wrinkled fist and proudly declared, "I am not a victim of gravity or criticism. I am a proud woman with a beautiful body, and you can kiss my attitude." I smiled and felt buoyant.

There are a few positive features of growing older, and one of the best examples is the absence of menstruation. No one misses that time of the month when we once traded white shorts for sensible black pants and endured bloating, cramping, and the occasional temptation to break something with a hammer. And, the men still don't understand and don't want to know what's happening. It's easier to joke about us being on the rag.

It didn't take 28 days for the 2016 political circus to get bloody awful. Two days after a televised debate, a male candidate insulted a feisty female news reporter by subtly remarking that she must be on her period. If our Founding Fathers had foreseen such ugly stains on their fertile new country, they would have grabbed the first protective vessel back to the motherland of England.

Men can get away with belching contests, lighting farts, and peeing on the golf course. Women bleed every month for 40 years and suffer from moodiness, cramps, bloating, and pain. Now their professionalism is questioned if they dare to be assertive. Personally, I'd rather trade activities with the men.

Polite and proper society never discusses menstruation, even though millions of women are having their periods right now. It's rarely portrayed in books, movies, or television shows, as if the natural phenomenon is too bloody awful to handle. Can you imagine if the character of a brave female astronaut or an intrepid pioneer woman or a sexy cabaret singer had to stop and fumble in her purse for a tampon? That would add a new meaning to the term "Ragtime."

Consider the word hysterical. Female hysteria was a once-common medical diagnosis, and its treatment was routine for many hundreds of years in Western Europe. In the medical literature of the nineteenth century, women considered to have the malady exhibited a wide array of symptoms and "a tendency to cause trouble." In extreme cases, the woman might be forced to enter an insane asylum or to undergo a surgical hysterectomy. That left plenty of time for the men to go camping, drink beer, and hunt animals. Or run for political office.

Many of us middle-aged women never received adequate information about having periods. Our bashful mothers handed us the blue Kotex box, an elastic belt, and a pamphlet with serious phrases such as:

"You're going to be a woman now, even though you're only 10."

"You will bleed every month for several decades from the Don't-Touch Area."

"There could be intense cramping, debilitating pain, and personal embarrassment, but no one wants to talk about it. Especially boys."

Nothing to fear, right? Our mother also worried about our ability to remain fresh and clean "down there." Ads from the fifties warned a woman that feminine odor could end their marriage! So, get out the Lysol and douche "the vaginal canal" if you want domestic bliss. Then you could use Lysol to clean the bathroom and really please your man.

At least we were better prepared with our daughters, and we gave them Judy Blume's wonderful 1970 book titled *Are You There, God? It's Me, Margaret.* Our daughters could identify with the excellent fictional account of a young girl having her first period. Of course, the book was banned in several schools and libraries because it was "sexually offensive and immoral." We've not progressed too far from medieval times when it comes to discussing periods.

In researching various websites including the Museum of Menstruation and Mental History, I discovered some interesting facts and added my own irreverent interpretation. In fertile females, their body prepares for pregnancy every month. When that doesn't happen, the uterus sheds its lining through blood and tissue. Missing a period can bring joy or fear, depending upon how much the woman wants to be pregnant.

During Biblical times, menstruating women were considered ritually impure and were required to be physically separated from men for the entire time they were bleeding. The men, meanwhile, continued to get drunk and kill each other. In England during the 1800s, *The British Medical Journal* published an article stating that menstruating women were medically unable to pickle meat, and in France, women on their periods couldn't work in sugar refineries because they would spoil the food. (And men wonder why we get moody! Go pickle your own damn meat.)

The first commercial sanitary pads were produced in the early 1900s, and an advertisement in 1921 showed women caring for a wounded soldier because in World War I French nurses noted that cellulose bandages used to treat wounds absorbed blood better than plain cotton. The Kotex ad rationalized that if the product was good enough for the military, it was good enough for mere women. Twenty years later in 1941, Kotex tossed the dutiful caretaker message and went straight for the gossiping women in swimsuits, and the caption, in discreet parentheses of course, said "The girls are talking about Tampons." Those scamps not only removed their humble nurse's outfits, they showed legs! Just imagine the fun times women had back then as they lolled around secretly chatting about tampons.

It only took another 21 years in 1962 for Pursettes brand of tampons to assure women that unmarried girls could safely and morally use their product. Apparently, there was fear that tampons would remove the virgin status of women, and as everyone knew, all unmarried women were virgins. Some cultures continue to penalize women. In the mountains of Nepal, menstruation is regarded as unclean so women are banished to small, bare huts. They should just accept their fate and plan a relaxing staycation. In sharp contrast, several Native American cultures consider a woman in menses to be at the height of her natural powers, and the Lakota tribe wouldn't allow a menstrual woman to come near the warriors because they feared her power would weaken their strength. Well played, Lakota women.

Menstruation will end if a woman reaches a certain age or has a complete hysterectomy. A hysterectomy that removed the ovaries can also result in immediate menopause, which brings a whole new collection of maladies, including moodiness, night sweats, exhaustion, forgetfulness, weight gain, and hair loss. But, look on the bright side. The money saved by not buying feminine products can go for therapy and/or wine. Call it a visit from Aunt Flo or The Curse or being On the Rag, women have survived their time of the month for thousands of years. They will continue to do so, because they're so tough and powerful. And, they can shine on prime time television during a political debate. Just ask the Lakota. Being fierce is admirable, but every now and then I secretly imagine what it would be like to have belching contests and light farts.

Just as we're celebrating the death of Aunt Flo, our bodies decide to mutiny in other ways. We adjust and endure the indignities of random mood swings and wrinkled skin that resembles a pricked balloon. Most of us regret that our eyesight isn't sharp anymore. With a pair of reading glasses perched on our head, and distance eyeglasses hanging around our neck while we wear contact lenses, we still squint to discern a bottle of eye drops from a bottle of super glue. The correct choice is imperative.

I would like to offer a clear plea, written in legible 12-point type, from middle-aged women to package designers.

Increase the size of the print on your products because our eyesight is weaker, our patience is shorter, and our brand loyalty is volatile. Give us big type or skip the hype because we're not buying it anymore.

There are more than 40 million middle-aged women in the United States, and we're irritated. Our buying power is estimated at $3 trillion dollars. That's trillion with a T. We don't care if you promise better, shinier, smoother, and more luxurious hair, we just want to decipher between shampoo and rinse without wearing eyeglasses in the shower.

I appreciate the elegant appearance of the most expensive brands, but I'd buy a case of dormitory-sized jugs of shampoo at Costco if the bottles contained labels in 24-point type. My less frustrated friends say to color-code the bottles, place the shampoo and rinse on different shelves, or add a colored band on one item. I reject that idea because then we let them win. If I pay almost ten dollars for a container of product, I shouldn't need to use any extra effort to identify it.

Visit any store and examine the labels. The wording on fingernail polish is a joke. We know how to use it, so why waste ink to print illegible pinpoint scribbles. The same goes for cosmetics. If I depended upon the words on the side of a makeup pencil, I wouldn't know if I should line my brows, eyelids, lips, or color a picture. I often see women who applied makeup without reading instructions, and I can only assume they also couldn't see close enough in the mirror to correct the mistakes.

Menus are maddening. The more expensive the restaurant, the more difficult the menu. Even with reading glasses and a spotlight, I can't decipher the tiny script so I'm forced to order a generic salad. Then I add an adult beverage and soon forget my frustration.

Books are blurry. Publishers attempt to save printing costs by reducing the size of the type so the book has fewer pages. However, I don't want to use eyeglasses and a magnifying glass to read past the first paragraph. The biggest advantage of e-readers and tablets is that we can adjust the size of the font.

Contracts are confusing. I suspect professionals use tiny print so the reader gets frustrated and signs the document. It's irritating when we're advised to read the small print and we can't even see the big title.

Reading theatre tickets annoys the masses. In a dimly lit performance hall, I can't see the row and seat numbers on the tickets so I need the assistance of a patient volunteer with a high-powered flashlight. This can be annoying to other patrons.

Recipes are ridiculous. So, the instructions really called for 1 teaspoon of garlic powder, not 1 cup. Teeny abbreviations in recipes can cause the cook to quit because of a ruined entrée and go to a fast-food restaurant where the items are displayed in huge, colored photographs. The food tastes like crap and has no nutritional value but at least you can see what you're ordering.

According to statistics provided at a recent conference on marketing to women, we control two-thirds of the consumer wealth in the United States. That should get the attention of small-minded designers. Just provide labels we can read. Easy enough? As an interesting side note, the same statistics revealed that middle-aged women account for 62 percent of vodka purchases. This is because we know what's in the bottle and how to use it.

Caveat: Manufacturers can reduce the size of print on bathroom scales. With this example, what we can't see won't hurt us.

~

Coloring Outside the Lines

One day I decided to take action and accomplish what any middle-aged woman would want to do: I ran away. After a hectic day of raising kids, working full-time, and trying to slap together three edible ingredients to make a family meal, I decided to ride away on a motorcycle. I depleted my saving account and bought a Harley-Davidson Custom Sportster, complete with extra chrome accessories, custom red paint, and fringed, leather saddle bags. I traded my heels for leather boots and felt the need for speed.

I completed a motorcycle safety course, the only middle-aged woman in a class full of slouching punks, goofy teenage boys, and old hippies. No one flirted with me or even muttered, "Hey, Babe. Let's take a walk on the wild side." I must have resembled their grandmother.

My first experiences riding my new motorcycle were exhilarating. I covered my head with a brain bucket, put the hammer down, and carved some serious curves while straddled upon 1200 ccs of unleashed power. I channeled my inner Steppenwolf to head out on the highway, looking for adventure, in whatever came my way. This liberated momma was bad to the bone.

"Ha!" I exclaimed after a month of riding into the wind. "I am an American legend!"

No one cared.

I made the obligatory trip to the Sturgis Motorcycle Rally in South Dakota. I felt sorry to see so many young women who were too poor to buy clothes. They ambled around wearing itty bitty leather thongs and fishnet tank tops. The poor things could barely walk upright due to the massive bouncing bosoms exploding from their tight leather vests. There was no way those bare butts ever sat more than five minutes on the back of a Harley.

My wild and crazy motorcycle days ended when I almost t-boned a mini-van full of children. I was cruising down a country road feeling free and festive when I noticed a minivan approaching from a side street. I knew where the driver was coming to a stop sign, but experience had taught me that those signs are often ignored. I watched but continued riding. The driver blew through the stop sign and pulled out directly in front of me. The vehicle was so close I could see the faces of children inside the car. Those sweet cherubs staring from the window were waiting for me to crash into their little bodies and leave my severed head beside the road.

I stomped on my foot brake, grabbed the hand brake, and swerved to the right. The bike stopped, but I didn't. I careened into the dirt, suddenly appreciating my heavy leather clothing. The driver never noticed and drove on down the road, oblivious to the yelling children. I hollered some uncharitable language and regrettably took the name of the Lord in vain while gesturing wildly like a possessed demon. These actions were not attractive.

The bike weighed more than 150 pounds, and I couldn't lift it. A group of motorcycle riders came along and stopped to help. They settled the bike upright, checked for damage, and offered to take me home. I gallantly refused any assistance and sent them on their way. I was pleased to see that the women in the biker group wore clothes.

I returned home and parked the bike. A few months later, I sold it to a man who always wanted a Harley. I wished him well and watched as he revved the engine.

"Watch out for distracted drivers of mini-vans," I yelled. "They're out to kill you!"

He waved back and I listened until the guttural noise from the V-twin engine faded in the distance. Returning to the house, I contently counted my cash and my blessings.

Several years after the motorcycle incident, I searched for another exciting outlet to express my creative side without getting wind in my hair or bugs in my teeth. The latest fad for inspiring peace and harmony was to use coloring books. Magazines and online websites noted that stressed people were using coloring books to relieve existential angst. Apparently, to supply the global demand, upscale retailers such as Yves Saint Laurent and Hermès offered adult coloring books for $160. For about the same cost, I would rather doodle on a napkin in a wine bar and enjoy a bottle of Quintessa Red Wine from Rutherford in Napa Valley.

"Just because everyone is doing it doesn't mean you need to do it," I was reminded of my mother's admonishments during my formative years. "If everyone jumped off a bridge, would you follow them?"

Mom wasn't too original in her advice strategy.

But, I never endorsed the popular addiction for adult coloring. Even as a wee child I didn't enjoy coloring because I couldn't stay within the lines. Never have, never will. Who can sit still when there are butterflies to chase, frogs to catch, and pebbles to toss into the pond?

In the spirit of positive adventure, I tried the free online samples. The outcome was disastrous. I concluded that I didn't have time for such shit. If other adults wanted to seek catharsis by way of colored pencils, that was fine with me. I agreed with professionals who claimed that art can be therapeutic. However, I was reminded of several artists through history who were not at peace with the universe or themselves.

Vincent Van Gogh was reported to be insane and depressed between manic bursts of creative energy. Pablo Picasso had issues as did Fransisco Goya and Salvador Dali. Famed artist Georgia O'Keeffe suffered an intense nervous breakdown and needed to stop painting for several years. And, who can forget Edvard Munch? It's been speculated that his famous painting of *The Scream* was a portal into his own anxiety, hallucinations, and subsequent psychotic breakdown.

I acknowledged that millions of adults were coloring and creating works of art in an attempt to soothe their troubled waters and find inner tranquility. That was fine with me. I just preferred to be left alone to self-medicate with a bold Cabernet. With respect to Van Gogh, I promised to not cut off my ear. That strategy worked well with my other convictions not to own another motorcycle. If learning from mistakes made a person wiser, I was the smartest person in the room.

~

The Joy of Traveling with (Grown) Children

If given the choice between traveling with small children and having a root canal, I'd be at the dentist's office sucking laughing gas before noon. I adore kids but the logistics of getting them more than 100 miles is too much to endure unless they can be shipped like golf clubs or crated like pets.

After my baby filled his diapers with an adult-strength load during takeoff on a three-hour flight, I finally realized there was no reason to ever travel with youngsters. At least not in the same airplane.

When my children were young, they didn't know what a vacation was, so I told them that the city park was just like Disneyland except without grinning pirates shooting guns, drinking booze, and chasing women on the Pirates of the Caribbean ride. Better yet, I turned on the sprinklers in the backyard, sat down with a glass of wine, and watched the little darlings giggle and wiggle until they were tired enough for a nap. Then I invited my hubby to swill some whiskey and chase me around the yard. Yo ho ho! Everyone was happy and we saved thousands of dollars. This was a win-win situation.

We finally made it to Disneyland when Emily was five and Adam was three, and we decided to give them the All-American family vacation. The distance between Boise, Idaho and Anaheim, California was 885 miles, so we calculated approximately 13 hours of driving time. Such foolish naivety! We forgot to schedule bathroom breaks every 30 minutes, time to stop and tell the kids to run around the car every hour, and unplanned detours due to roadwork and failure to correctly read the map.

My husband was driving and we were finally getting close to Anaheim. We were driving in frantic rush-hour traffic when Emily declared the sentence parents dread.

"I have to go potty."

"Just hold it, Honey. We're almost there," I lied. The exit for the hotel was a mile away and we were surrounded by half the vehicles in southern California.

"I can't hold it anymore. It's going to come out!"

I frantically pawed through the travel bags and pulled out a can of potato chips, the kind that are stacked so neatly. I hated those chips. I came from generations of Idaho potato farmers, so I knew that the ingredients contained more rice, wheat, and corn byproducts than potatoes. Without a second thought, I dumped the contents on the floor and I held out the can for her.

"Look! You can go potty in this can! Won't that be fun?"

"I can't," she cried. "Make him stop looking."

"Adam," I instructed my son. "Look out the window. Now." I wiggled around from the passenger seat to the back seat and helped her push down her pants and underwear. Then we positioned the potato chip can at just the correct place and she filled it almost to the brim.

"You did it!" I exclaimed. We all cheered. I handed her some tissues, poked them into the can, and secured the lid. That can of urine made it safely to the next exit where it was deposited in the nearest trash receptacle along with the heap of chips from the floor. To this day, no one in the family has purchased that particular brand of chips.

We enjoyed Disneyland and the fun for us was watching our kids get so excited when they hugged the "real" Snow White or the "real" Pluto. Adam was a fan of Donald Duck, and it happened to be Donald Duck's 50th Birthday Parade. He stood throughout the entire parade, alternately waving and clutching his chest in total amazement. That's a memory I'll never forget. I wanted someone to look at me like my son looked at Donald Duck.

Reality set in when we packed up the kids and the car to drive back to Idaho. Only 885 miles to go. It seemed like a journey half way around the world. We weren't out of California before the whining started from the back seat. At this stage, bribery is the only choice for parents.

"Please stop whining and you can have a new puppy/pony/playhouse if we get home before you're in high school."

After spending the mortgage at Disneyland and driving four more hours through a desolate desert listening to a cacophony of quarrels between the siblings, I finally turned around and snarled like a possessed maniac.

"Stop hitting each other or I will park this car right now and we'll live off the land and eat scorpions until you can learn to behave."

That appeased the little darlings for an hour.

When it was my turn to drive, the trip became a matter of survival. I was so exhausted I no longer cared who was in the car or where we were going. My husband fell asleep, and after hours of hearing "Are we there yet?" and "How much longer?" I chose to take my own personal vacation and played a fun game of charades.

"Sorry kids. Mommy is going away for a while."

Then I pulled over to a secure rest stop along the road, turned off the car, closed my eyes, and played dead for at least ten minutes. That clever technique worked every time.

We eventually arrived home, and I kissed the ground. The kids tumbled into the house with their packages, official mouse ear hats, and other assorted treasures. The next day, we organized our prized possessions and they played quietly in their rooms for at least 30 minutes. Then one of them came out and said, "I'm bored." In hindsight, I'm ashamed of the wicked way I stabbed my good throw pillow with a steak knife.

The first time I saw the movie *The Sound of Music* I yelled "Fraud!" at the end as the family climbed over the Alps singing in perfect harmony in clean clothes. When my kids were little, we couldn't walk from the house to the car without someone falling headfirst into a mud puddle. And forget about taking a hike together. Any incline more than two inches would cause howls of dismay with repeated pleas to be carried. And that's when they were teenagers! But, in deference to the movie, if evil Nazis were chasing us, we would manage to escape together, with or without matching lederhosen.

When I became an older curmudgeon, I snickered when I saw young parents in airports juggling a small mountain of luggage that included diapers, food, enormous strollers, DVD players, toys, and clothes that could stock a child care center.

"My ancestors walked for months to Idaho along the Oregon Trail, and their kids and clothes were bathed once a week in the river, air-dried on a log, and stored in the wagon for the day's journey," I said to my friend Linda as we prepared to board an airplane for a business trip to Arizona. "They survived just fine."

"Don't criticize those frazzled young parents too much or you could get a screaming toddler dumped in your lap," Linda said. "It's best to smile and help, if necessary."

"I know you're right. But just imagine if any pioneer child had complained."

"Pa, the wagon's too bumpy!"

"Hush, Child, and go trap a rabbit, skin it, and help your Ma make dinner. We're walking ten miles tomorrow."

We laughed, helped a struggling mother with adjusting her front pack full of baby and bags, and boarded the plane. Though some kid was kicking the back of my seat during the entire flight, I kept calm, knowing when we landed I could easily get off the plane and survive the day without herding a tired gang of kids.

One splendid advantage of getting older is that family trips are easier and less hectic. My kids are in their thirties and have their own children to handle, so I just need to pack yoga pants, t-shirts, and a wine opener. We recently traveled with 11 family members on a week-long vacation to Mexico. We stayed at a family resort on the ocean and took turns sharing responsibilities for keeping the children within screaming distance. I was overjoyed to play with the grandkids and sing songs and tell stories. Then came Happy Hour and their parents could take over.

During the trip, we decided to test the limits for patience and adaptability by arranging a family photograph. Reunions and vacations are ideal times to stop all the fun, force people to wear matching clothes, and pose for hours in unnatural positions. It's an extra challenge if there is a fussy baby who would rather be home taking a nap in her crib.

Six adults and five children bravely attempted the portrait on a trip to a resort by the ocean. We erroneously scheduled the photograph for late afternoon to capture the sun setting over the sea. Any future family pictures will be scheduled for early morning before the sun, ocean, and tequila have altered the moods of all involved. The kids had played all day on the beach, obtaining varying degrees of sunburn despite gallons of sunscreen slathered every two minutes over their bodies. The adults took turns watching the kids and consuming tasty drinks decorated with tiny umbrellas. A few were dozing when my daughter-in-law announced that we had 30 minutes to get ready for the photographer. Cries were heard, and not from the children.

The instructions were to wear clothes in various shades of blue. That seemed a simple requirement, but the day before the photos, three girls aged five, seven, and nine decided they wanted matching dresses. The mothers left two babies with the fathers and took the rest of the brood into town, searching the shops for inexpensive outfits. It was impossible to find matching dresses in three sizes and after a few hours we were tempted to bribe them with alternative suggestions.

"If you wore different colors, you could look like a rainbow!" exclaimed my daughter. "Then we could get ice cream."

The girls weighed the choice and burst into tears, wailing that they wanted matching dresses *and* ice cream. I stepped back and watched the mothers practice parenting techniques that ran the gamut from positive cajoling to finally threatening to sell the girls as fishmongers to the fishermen at the wharf. Again, I enjoyed my role as supportive older woman who no longer had youngsters. We were heading to the nearest cantina when the five-year-old squealed with delight. She saw a tiny shop tucked in an alley with countless blue dresses fluttering in the breeze. We found three matching dresses in the exact sizes. It was a spiritual event.

Later that night, after the five children were tucked into bed, the adults sat on the patio sipping appropriate resort beverages and discussed the important decisions of the day. One father remarked that he wanted sea bass for dinner, the other asked if anyone was ready to go in a glass-bottom boat the next day, and my husband suggested a spa appointment for a massage. Apparently, they missed the memo that they needed to focus on another pressing issue.

"What are you wearing for the family photo?" my daughter asked.

The men looked at her and at each other. I could tell they were mentally calculating if they should laugh or feign concern. They chose the best response.

"Of course," my son said. "I've been thinking about that all day."

"Didn't you say blue?" asked my son-in-law. "I'm wearing a white shirt and blue shorts."

"Me, too," said my son, considering the case closed. "Now, about that sea bass."

My daughter and daughter-in-law weren't satisfied yet. They wanted to be sure the white shirts were clean, that the men knew the appointed time and place, and who would take responsibility for the various children. My husband and I sat back and winked at each other.

Finally, it was the appropriate date and hour for the photograph. The kids were dragged from the beach, showered, dressed, and combed. The adults straggled to their rooms and prepared for the major event. The eight females all wore blue dresses, two men wore white shirts and blue shorts, and my husband wore a blue shirt and shorts. We resembled a school choir group from the 1980s.

The activity took over an hour and the poses were more calculated than portrait sessions for most weddings. Each family was photographed, then the children, then the couples, then everyone together, smiling with great joy. We sat on the stairs, in the grass, on a whitewashed bench, and finally on the beach in front of the ocean. By this time, the baby was crying, the three-year-old refused to smile, the three other girls were doing cartwheels in the sand, and my husband kept pinching my butt. Finally, the session was over, the photographer left, and our blue group paraded to our rooms to find shade and comfort. A group of spectators clapped politely.

The next day we hurried to the customer service desk to view the photographs. We had originally agreed to purchase the Limited Package, featuring six large and twelve small photos. By the time we giggled and gushed over every single picture, I broke down and bought the entire Deluxe Family Memory Package for only $250. The group picture of all of us stretched hand-in-hand on the beach in front of the ocean remains my favorite photo of all time. It was, indeed, the deluxe family memory.

The rest of the vacation went well, due to the lack of organized activities with required dress codes, until the day we were to leave for the airport. My family knows that traveling with me could at any moment include a frantic dash to the nearest restroom, so stay out of the way. I inherited my mother's positive attitude, pragmatic work ethic, and irritable bowel syndrome. If she left home for more than an hour, she carried medication to either stop diarrhea or relieve constipation. Her days and movements were regulated more than her bowels. I thought it was normal to anticipate digestive calamites and was always pleasantly surprised if my travels didn't include at least one potentially humiliating event.

As the family gathered at the airport, the parents went down the checklist: backpacks on, snacks included, liquids out, passports ready. Inevitably the parents would ask if everyone, including me, had gone potty. We all nodded and promised we had. Only I received a skeptical look from the other adults. I was slightly offended, but went again to find the restroom. I'm a people-pleaser like that.

All eleven of us got onto the plane and settled into our assigned seats. Just as the airplane began to taxi for liftoff, I felt the evil gurgle on the left side of my body. Those damn demons. I knew I wouldn't be able to hold what was coming, so I had to act instantly. I unbuckled my belt and rushed to the back of the plane. One flight attendant attempted to intercept me, but I refused to stop and locked myself in the bathroom. Just as the plane left the ground, I experienced an unusual euphoria as I sat unbuckled and uninhibited in a tiny, windowless room and eliminated a great deal of stress. I didn't come out until the flight was well underway.

No one questioned as I made my way back to my seat because they knew my unauthorized action had been a gallant act of courtesy to everyone. I smiled as I watched another middle-age woman charge toward the bathroom. We belonged to a strong sisterhood of women who suffer from body betrayal but are still brave enough to leave our houses.

Traveling with grown children and their families required precise logistics, patience, money, a love of adventure, and most important, a sense of humor. If the same number of people returned as the same number of people who left, it was considered a successful journey. I framed and displayed the photograph of the happy family stretched across the beach in front of the ocean. The portrait proved that my children survived their unpredictable childhood with me to become good people with loving families. I made a plan to invite myself along on all future adventures. I was confident they would be delighted.

Our airplane landed safely, and we gathered to collect our luggage and hug goodbye before going our separate ways. As we walked away with the boisterous brood, I overheard one of my adult children say, "Stop hitting your sister or we'll go live in the desert and eat scorpions until you learn to behave." My work was done.

~

Tell Enchanting Stories to the Grandkids

"Please tell me a made-up story, Tutu," my wee granddaughter I call Baby Boo begged as I closed her picture book and tucked her into bed. I mentally scrambled for an image and suddenly a little old lady popped into my imagination.

"Here's one," I said, much to her delight. Then I began the spontaneous tale of a sad older lady who needed an adventure. I tossed in the ability to fly and to find magical meadows with talking birds. It always helped to include at least one princess, a nasty troll, and a few immature bodily noises. For a successful story that pleased the most discerning child, I relied upon past experience: A flying princess, yes. Dead puppies, no.

I thought of a few more stories, and each story became more elaborate with magical places and outlandish characters. Then she asked me to repeat the first ones. Of course, I couldn't remember the exact plots. I made a mental note to record or write down future stories so I wouldn't forget. It was interesting that my granddaughter had remembered details of the story long after I had told it to her. When she reminded me in one repeated story that the little girl had ridden a unicorn to an enchanted forest and had not been carried there by a magic bird, I quickly adapted the scenario. Such was the hazard of spontaneous storytelling.

My skills to imagine and tell tall tales came from being a childhood daydreamer. I spent the better part of 5th grade staring out of the classroom window on the third floor of an old school building in Wendell, Idaho. My endless daydreams were an irritation to my teacher Mrs. Gates, but I earned good grades so she couldn't complain. I yearned to seek adventures and tell stories of life beyond the limitations of the dusty blackboard and the hard wooden seat.

I studied clouds, and watched the traffic coming and going; trucks pulling flatbed trailers with farm equipment, tankers of diesel heading for surrounding farms, long trailers full of cattle, pickup trucks loaded with hay bales and dogs, and occasional sedans. I wondered about the people scurrying below as I imagined grand adventures. After pondering the world beyond my classroom, I often wrote poems and short stories on my Big Chief Tablet. Most of the adults in my life considered this activity a waste of time, so I kept pages of written words in shoe boxes in my closet. They became my private stash of contraband, but they propelled me to keep writing.

During my volatile teenage years, music was my salvation as I listened to The Monkees sing "Daydream Believer" and the Lovin' Spoonful sing "What a Day for a Daydream." As a college student, my first car was a Firebird and I drove around feeling groovy as an eight-track tape in my car played Aretha Franklin singing "Daydreaming." Music continued to prompt spontaneous fantasies, and I grew fond of an eclectic variety of tunes: "Go West" by the Pet Shop Boys, "Song for a Winter's Night" by Sarah McLachlan, and anything by Tina Turner.

The dictionary describes daydreaming as "a short-term detachment from reality when one's surroundings were substituted by a visionary fantasy, especially one of happy, pleasant thoughts, hopes or ambitions." Anyone who ever sat through a boring lecture or drove a long distance through barren scenery knows the value of short-term detachment. I've missed several exits along various journeys through life because my driving concentration was distracted by visionary fantasies. That last chance for gas sign was totally ignored as I drove along thinking about make-believe conversations in fictional places. I know there is a medical prescription to deal with delusions, but I prefer to keep my imaginary friends. They don't get dramatic, won't get upset if I forget their birthday, and they never borrow my favorite shirt and trash it like my former real friend did.

When I grew up, the art of daydreaming was criticized for being nonproductive and even dangerous. According to a study published in *Psychology Today,* a researcher named Eric Klinger noted that some educational psychologists in the 1950s warned parents not to let their children daydream for fear that the children would be sucked into neurosis and psychosis. With all due respect, that's bullshit.

Once after jumping on the trampoline with Baby Boo, I begged her to stop before my bladder prolapsed. We laid on the trampoline and watched the clouds, finding yawning alligators, a long-eared rabbit, and a three-eyed snake.

"Why don't the clouds fall down," she asked in her five-year-old curiosity.

"They're held in the sky by millions of flying fairies who take turns because they live in the clouds," I answered because I was too lazy to explain how clouds are formed. Flying fairies are much more exciting.

"Tell me about how they live in the clouds, Tutu."

"Well, each cloud holds a different city. That one over there has the bakery and makes cookies for all the fairies. That big cloud is full of fairy children who play in the park and ride baby unicorns. See the long, dark cloud? That's the time-out place for naughty fairies."

Sometimes I amuse myself with my own stories. I have no idea where they come from or what's coming next, but I let them wander about awhile. I include plenty of positive, wonderful scenarios but every now and then a rogue element appears.

"Oh no. It looks like two little fairies are fighting. I hope they don't tumble off the cloud and crash to the ground!"

"What happened?" Baby Boo was worried.

"Oh, good news. A little fairy named Baby Boo came over and stopped the fight just as they were about to fall down. Everything is fine again on the children's cloud."

Baby Boo was satisfied.

"Let's go inside and get cookies," she said. "Then you can tell me more stories."

I enjoy my role as a storyteller, and I love how the process sparks my aging abilities to think and pretend. I own a small collection of ceramic storytellers crafted in Peru and New Mexico. They're shaped from clay to resemble a woman surrounded by children. They represent the South American and Native American Indian tradition of using oral stories as a teaching tool for younger generations.

The figurines include a centered, nurturing, and powerful woman who inspires the children with lessons and stories about their culture. The attempt to entertain my children and grandchildren through stories has an added benefit because the activity helps prevent my brain from turning into mush.

Over the years, I developed techniques for how to tell an enchanting story. First, I begin with a provocative set-up: One day a little girl/puppy/mother/King woke up and discovered that no one was home. Then I explain how something happened, either to the main character or the environment. For example, the princess searched in all the rooms but no one was there. On the kitchen table, she saw a bright red arrow pointing to the back yard.

In one or two phrases, I tell how the plot thickened and the drama was raised when tension appeared: She peeked out the window and saw a fairy/pony/rainbow/salesman/monster/dead fish. I analyze the reaction of the audience and adjust accordingly. If the listeners aren't engaged by that time, I strengthen the narrative: The character was afraid/surprised/happy/shy/vomiting/eating her arm.

The next step is to craft a vision of a scene that involves the senses of sight, sound, taste, vision, and touch: The door creaked as she opened it and tiptoed barefoot in her calico gown into the cool grass. She felt a gentle breeze toss her red hair, and the air smelled of mint and oranges. Those embellishments weave a story with a climax that produces a positive reaction from the listeners. Suddenly the little girl's family appeared with gifts for her surprise party. Or, for a more creative tale, she followed a cluster of chaotic clowns as they scampered over a slippery rainbow into a secret castle full of toys, sugar cookies, and singing vegetables.

I finish when the story is resolved. It was the perfect surprise party. Or, she loved her imaginary friends and promised to join them again another day. Or, she scurried home to read adventure books and plan her next excursion. To improve my storytelling abilities, I recorded myself reciting an original fable. That technique allowed me to pace my telling of the story and to eliminate too many pauses or unnecessary words, such as *um* or *you know.*

Some people are born to be storytellers, and their yarns and tall tales aren't limited to children. They often regale adults with their creative stories, and a friendly bar or boisterous camping trip only intensifies the renditions. For centuries, well-told narrations have enriched the imaginations of children and entertained adults. As an added benefit, the regular practice keeps the brain energized so the speakers are ready any time a small voice begs, "Please, tell me a story."

~

My Views from Behind the Podium

"Thanks for taking time out of your busy schedule to be here. I've had company for a month! I finally took my aunt to the airport this morning, but now I'm feeling guilty. Her plane doesn't leave until next week."

Then I wait for the audience to laugh. If they respond with loud guffaws, I feel like a comedic genius and breeze into the rest of the speech. If they fake a bored smile, I know they've repressed their inner clown and it's my duty to set them free. I focus on the grumpiest person and mentally make a mission to evoke at least an audible chuckle. It's a silly mind game I play simultaneously while my mouth is talking. Here's an example of the conversation going on in my head.

See the lady in the brown suit? The one scowling at me?

Yes. She thinks you're stupid. Get off the stage now and go home.

Ha! Give me five minutes. I'll make her laugh.

Give up, Honey. You passed your prime years ago.

Wait. She liked that last joke. Look. There's a grin. Ha! She laughed! I win.

You better ratchet up the delivery. There's a snoozer in the third row.

I often begin speeches and workshop presentations with the aunt to the airport joke because it usually provokes laughter from the audience. Why? First, people can identify with being busy and they appreciate a welcome for attending. Second, they understand the duties of dealing with house guests. Third, there is an unexpected twist at the end. You can substitute aunt with mother-in-law, depending upon the strength of your marriage and assuming she's not in the audience.

So far, no one has booed, thrown rotten fruit, or had me arrested. The audience knows I'm joking, but they laugh anyway because it's a funny scenario. If no one laughs, I know it will be a tough audience so I mentally prepare to tap dance, light my hair on fire, or clutch my chest and stumble off the stage. If it's an easy crowd, I immediately add a second image.

"My sweet aunt was sick last year, so I visited her. She was in bed, and as we talked I munched on peanuts in a bowl on her nightstand. After I had eaten all the peanuts, I offered to buy more. She said she couldn't eat peanuts because they hurt her teeth. She just sucked off the chocolate and put them back in the bowl."

That story also guarantees a laugh because the audience can see my aunt sick in bed and feels tender support for my visit. Then the silly image of her sucking off the chocolate hits their funny bone. For added emphasis, I use a southern drawl for my aunt's voice. It's all in great fun and causes the group to relax and prepare for my speech. In a few minutes, we've become best friends and will soon share social media accounts. "What's your Twitter handle?" is the new "What's your zodiac sign?" Without a humorous introduction, it would take more time to connect with the listeners. Also, speakers are energized by a positive reaction from the audience, and it's like an extra bonus to have people in the front row laughing boisterously at every anecdote. For professional credibility, these people should be sober.

Caveat: don't read jokes, and don't tell them if you're not comfortable with public speaking. Rehearse the stories out loud so you get the timing and phrasing correct. A well-delivered punch line to an original anecdote can be a golden experience as the audience reacts and instantly loves you. Conversely, a dull, lifeless and insecure presentation is painful for everyone. Make sure the joke is not on you.

I speak at conferences and writing workshops and often include assorted props and gimmicks to enhance the presentations. I stand stoically as the airport security staff paws through my bag of finger puppets, bells, clown noses, tambourines, and a petrified turtle's egg. When they question the contents, I reply that I'm performing at the White House, or on Broadway, or at the funeral of a famous clown who was trampled to death by a rogue elephant. I receive instant clearance.

Speaking at the Erma Bombeck Writers' Workshop was one of the top highlights of my career. I packed 300 finger puppets, a collection of new jokes, and some sensible shoes to travel to the conference in Dayton, Ohio. I use the puppets to show the audience how to transfer negative, insecure thoughts to the puppets while inviting them to provide charming, positive encouragement. It's great fun to cause stuffy engineers to turn into silly schoolboys singing rounds in perfect harmony while using their empowered finger puppets. These cheap but powerful props are available in bulk at party stores or online, and I advise people to keep a few at their desks as a distraction from grouchy people or in their car to wiggle at the driver in the next car while stopped at a light. You might want to lock your door.

To prepare for the Erma Bombeck talk, I studied the conference website and created stories and anecdotes to tailor and enhance the message for the group. The conference was scheduled at the University of Dayton where an astute professor once told his student Erma Bombeck, "You can write!" My presentation titled "Write Funny, NOW!" included quotes from Bombeck's material and incorporated writing prompts. Twenty years after her death, Bombeck remains the super star and role model for female humor writers.

The first rule of most communication is to know your audience, and the majority of attendees were women who write humor. Bingo. That group was so much better than a convention of fortune tellers and psychics because they would know the punch lines.

The Bloggers at Midlife Conference in Las Vegas featured panel discussions and workshops to teach techniques for monetizing blogs, expanding social media contacts, improving writing skills, and publishing blogs into books. Almost all of the attendees were women, so the trade show sponsors included cosmetic lines, life insurance companies, and a website that helps worried parents find dates for their grown children. To gain material for my speech, I listened to the conversations during registration and made notes on which people and stories to exploit.

Every now and then I get a few people in the audience who challenge my good will. Despite advance warning, some people will talk or text on a cell phone. I'll stop and stare at them until they shut off the phone. Some people go to sleep, and that's okay as long as they're quiet. At one workshop, a lady started snoring so I walked past her and wiggled her knee. She snorted awake and pretended nothing had happened. I've seen passionate young couples pressed together, so inspired by my motivational words that they hold hands and sigh. It's the least I can do.

One awkward conversation occurred as I was speaking to a group about blogging.

"What's a blog?" yelled a woman from the back of the room as I was midway into the presentation. I remained positive.

"Our topic today is how experienced bloggers can publish their blogs," I said. "I can talk with you after the session."

"Just tell me how I can start a blog!"

Several audience members cringed. They hadn't paid for the workshop to discuss something they already knew.

"I can meet you after the session."

"Well, I don't have time for that," she said, gathering her materials and marching for the door. She stalled at the door and hollered, "Thanks for nothing!" Then she exited the room.

Those in the room gasped in unison, and I knew a sour interruption would ruin the flow. I grabbed a finger puppet and wiggled it as I said in my best imitation of the Southern drawl used in the prison warden's famous quote in *Cool Hand Luke*, "What we've got here is failure to communicate."

The audience loved the response and we continued uninterrupted with our workshop. I searched later but never found the woman. I was prepared to share with her some elementary blogging details. Perhaps she found a better workshop that involved crafts and glue guns and free prizes so she couldn't say 'thanks for nothing.'

For those who want to incorporate humor in their public speaking, I offer three main tips. First, turn off the news. Balance your intake with funny shows, movies, books, and silly friends. Second, avoid crabby people. They're everywhere. Hang out with those who like to laugh. Finally, practice laughter. Read daily positive, humorous affirmations and focus on all the good stories.

Laughter is good for the body and soul. And, a sense of humor provides a great way to make and keep friends. As the American author and humorist Mark Twain said, "Humor is the great thing, the saving thing. The minute it crops up, all our irritation and resentments slip away and a sunny spirit takes their place."

I returned from the conference in time to present a humorous speech to a group of executive women in Boise. My confidence was high as I wiggled into my dress, gathered my notes, and sashayed to my car with 45 minutes to make a 30-minute drive. That's when I was reminded that the best intentions can be blown apart in a moment. The tire on my car was flat.

I take pride in handling each crisis but there are two chores I refuse to learn: how to change a tire and how to use a chainsaw. There are other people who can do those activities far better than I can. And, everyone knows I would cut off at least one appendage if I ever held anything that involved buzzing sharp edges. I buy Band-Aids in bulk because I've been known to slice through skin with a dull butter knife. Chainsaws are for loggers and horror movies.

I glared at the flat tire and calculated my options. My husband was at work 40 minutes away. My adult children were all on vacation. My neighbors were gone, and my town didn't have a taxi service. I called Uber, but the nearest driver was an hour away. I called the woman who had invited me to speak and left a desperate message of apology on her voice mail. Then I called the private club and left another anxious message. By then, it was time to be at the presentation.

An important rule to know: When all else fails, try Facebook. I frantically logged into my account online and issued a global plea for a ride. Instantly, friends responded so I took the closest one. I arrived an hour late to the event, but by then all the guests were on their second cocktail and feeling quite forgiving and jovial. They laughed with me before my first joke, and that's when I finally was able to breathe without whimpering.

So, I stood before the group with Monster Puppet telling me in one ear that I was a loser and no one would ever ask me to speak again. He even said my dress was ugly. Queen Puppet responded with positive affirmations that shit happens and I glow brighter than the morning sun. The banter continued until Monster Puppet ultimately was vanquished. The speech moved into my prepared remarks and ended with applause. Merriment and more drinks ensued.

I begged a ride home and made plans to contact the tire dealer. As I prepared for bed, Monster Puppet snarled that I was too stupid and lazy to learn how to change a tire. Queen Puppet suddenly appeared with a chainsaw and chopped off his head. Unfortunately, my finger was cut again.

I distribute finger puppets after most of my presentations, and people take them home or to their offices to remind themselves to seek humor in mundane situations. My friend Jennifer was a customer service representative for a large technology firm. Though her dreams and aspirations never included sitting in a padded cubicle listening to rude customers, that's what she did for eight hours a day. Usually, the problems were related to consumer ignorance, and she would patiently instruct them to put in a battery or plug the device into an electrical outlet. To keep her sanity, she used a collection of finger puppets on her desk and pretended the callers were puppets. Then she could see and talk to the clown or the pig or the snooty lady bouncing on her finger. She used humor to survive.

Jennifer left that job as she approached midlife. Her children were grown, her husband had retired to the golf course, and she wanted more time for herself. She packed up her finger puppets and found a part-time job in the children's ward of a local hospital. She left obnoxious customers to work with a captive audience of kids with real problems. Her biggest reward was making them laugh.

From Shakespeare to the comic strip character Dilbert, ordinary characters rely on comedy to endure the struggles of life and death. As Mercutio lies dying in the tragedy of *Romeo and Juliet* his last words are, "A plague on both your houses! They have made worm's meat of me!" Then he laughs and dies. That's a morbidly funny line. Worm's meat? Would that really be a man's last thought? Shakespeare is playing with the audience so the tragedy won't be too horrific.

In the passionate and wildly popular Broadway musical *Les Miserables,* we're exhausted as we witness the endless pain and terrible turmoil of characters who just want to live one more day to fulfill their destiny. Then just before we sink into a deep depression, the drunken innkeeper and his wife burst onto the stage with a hilarious rendition of "Master of the House." The audience cheers with gratitude for the temporary emotional reprieve.

In a favorite Dilbert cartoon, the intern Asok is killed and reincarnated as a candy bar. Office workers can relate to Asok, but the episode made us laugh anyway. Why? We're amused because nothing diffuses daily drama like a boisterous belly laugh. Studies prove laughter can reduce stress, increase creativity, and lessen tensions. Happy people are healthier than crabby people, and they're a lot more fun to be around. Jovial people can tackle problems with a positive attitude while pessimistic whiners only take up space while wasting time and life by drafting hate mail and threatening law suits.

Just in case you meet or work with nasty people who only exist to bring pain and suffering to the world, here are some suggestions for using humor to diffuse stressful situations.

Before going to a serious meeting, walk by an outside playground and listen to the laughter of the children. Try to recapture that exuberant feeling of having fun. You don't have to install a swing set in your office to remember how it feels to swing high and almost touch the clouds.

Cheerfully empathize with people who drive you crazy. Maybe the coworker who criticizes your work has an intolerable life at home or is caring for a sick child. That would explain his or her irritating behavior. Or, the coworker could just be truly obnoxious and you should stay away from that person as much as possible. If you're in a tense meeting and tempers are flaring, stand up and wave a white flag. Threaten to send everyone to "time out" if they can't get along. Your boss may not approve of your actions, but it could lighten the mood.

If you're unfortunate enough to be placed on a rigid committee that can't find consensus on anything, carry a jester's hat in your briefcase. As emotions escalate and you'd rather break for lunch, just don the hat and announce that you are Feste the Fool of Shakespeare's *Twelfth Night.* Dramatically sing his immortal line: "Come away, come away death!" You'll all be laughing your way through the lunch line.

If you're cursed enough to be deemed in charge of the office holiday party, know in advance that you cannot please everyone and that you are doomed to failure. Just emulate the television show *Seinfeld.* During one politically correct episode, they organized a "Festivus for the Rest of Us" party where they celebrated nothing. It worked.

Share the joy by driving to work wearing a clown nose. At the stoplight, look over and smile at the people in the next car. You'll brighten their day because they'll laugh on their way to work, or else they'll report you to the police. That's okay because the noses come off quickly. Employ popular tricks and tactics that you use with your family to improve negative situations at work. If your assistant gets an important report done on time, give him an extra-long lunch hour. Legal bribery works wonders, and you're both happier.

Never forget that there are people who want you to be miserable. They may want your job or your car or your spouse. They will publicly criticize you and make your life miserable. Just laugh at the situation and be thankful the person isn't your parent. However, if it is your parent, get some professional therapy. Also never forget that there are people who want you to be happy. You should belong to some social, professional, or civic organizations where you can mingle with supportive people who share your values, skills and aspirations. Just ignore Groucho Marx's famous comment that he would never belong to a club that would have him as a member.

Silence is goal-oriented. While it can be fun to slay the competition with a well-placed witticism, sometimes it's best to pick your battles, remain silent, and allow the adversary to publicly prove that she's a fool. If she goes into a tirade, concentrate on her left ear and imagine it's a donkey's ear. You will look cool, calm, and collected while she self-destructs faster than the Wicked Witch of the West. You can make your sly comments after you're promoted.

The best advice is to know that if you're wallowing with the pigs, get out of the sty. You don't have to tolerate uncomfortable, hostile, or abusive treatment, and if you're not occasionally laughing at work, you can't work. Consider a department change or pursue educational opportunities for advancement. If you're going to live to be 100, you might as well enjoy the journey. And don't forget to pack your sense of humor.

For some reason, probably budget problems or because someone forgot to get a speaker, I've been the commencement speaker for the University of Idaho, the College of Southern Idaho, and several high schools. Before each speech, I create inspirational, twenty-minute messages to convince clueless graduates that life will be great if they just get a job, floss daily, and call their mom once a week.

On the other hand, I could tell them they are doomed, there aren't any jobs, the country is on the brink of destruction, they'll never get out of debt and they should move into the woods and make wool macramé hangers to sell at craft fairs. But that advice might not motivate them to attain their potential greatness.

Thousands of graduates and their families sit through commencement ceremonies each spring, and I hope they glean a few tidbits of wisdom from the speakers who will desperately be searching for eye contact. It's difficult for motivational speakers to keep going when they know the audience already has checked out. In between the pomp and the circumstance, I tried my best to offer some simple suggestions for a good life:

Accept the fact that life isn't fair. You could work hard, excel at your job and miss your kid's school programs, only to have your job eliminated or discover the business is a front for organized crime. Or you could get hit by a beer truck or your spouse could run away with a carnival worker or your hillbilly neighbor could get a lucrative reality show on television. Just grit your teeth, change your profession, and write country/western songs.

No one owes you a living. Chances are, you're not going to win the Publisher's Clearinghouse Sweepstakes or the million-dollar lottery. And you can't live with your parents anymore, because they want to buy a recreational vehicle and travel around to casinos and roadside attractions. Go into the world and make your own way. Be sure to send photos to your mom, wherever she is.

Take risks. Watch children if you need examples of expert risk-takers. Kids love to stomp in puddles, fall out of trees, catch frogs in a ditch, and ride anything with wheels. Be like they are and experience true freedom before life gives you a mortgage, kids, in-laws, fifty extra pounds, buffoon bosses, and irritable bowel syndrome.

Mansions, fast cars, and luxury vacations don't guarantee happiness. Many good people are honestly delighted to have a small house with indoor plumbing, a pickup truck that runs, a pantry full of homemade food, and a favorite camping place. Be like that.

Get out of debt. Why work your entire life just to pay interest to a bank? In most cases, that $100 debt on your credit card for that sassy pair of boots will remain long after they have worn out. Pay cash or go bootless.

I told graduates at the College of Southern Idaho to avoid student loans because the devious program would make them indebted to the government for several decades. I could tell by their groans that the warning came too late. So I advised their younger siblings in the audience to investigate other financial aid options, including scholarships, grants, work-study programs, or trade schools. These students will have homes and new trucks while their older brothers and sisters will be living in a crowded commune while paying on their endless student loans.

Enjoy relationships. The happiest people are surrounded by family members and friends who accept their faults, celebrate their achievements, and invite them over for barbecues and beer.

Avoid crabby people. They will suck out every last ounce of your energy and leave you a withered, bitter shell of wretched humanity. Purge your contact list now before it's too late.

Don't fight. No explanation needed.

Love more. Ditto.

Laugh, dance, and sing. Triple ditto.

I purposely avoided any mention of politics or religion, because I'd rather smack my head with a hammer than tiptoe through the minefield of political correctness. I always conclude my speech with this last bit of advice: Call your mom and thank her for putting up with you. If she's no longer living, call another mother and wish her a happy day. You'll both feel good, and the world needs more people who are truly grateful.

To complement the speaking activities, I often conduct retreats that incorporate music and writing. The workshop invites participants to listen to various songs and then spontaneously write using the music as the only prompt. This muse always inspires creative results in a range of emotions from melancholy to stand-up-and-holler joyful.

I've used this technique to teach adults and school children. In my collection of vintage books, I have a copy of a children's book from 1886 titled *Please Tell Me A Tale.* One story, "Under the Maypole", has the following lines:

This Mayday morning they will plant the Maypole on the green,

And hang it round with cowslip wreaths and blue bells set between;

With starry thorn, with knotted fern, with chestnut blossoms tall,

And Phil, the bailiff's son, will bring red roses from the Hall.

Can't you just imagine little Phil proudly bringing the roses? The book doesn't have any illustrations, but children still love to listen to the lyrical stories and imagine the scenes.

I use this example in my writing class for local fourth grade students. Then I follow with an excerpt from a current bestselling children's book, *Captain Underpants and the Perilous Plot of Professor Poopypants.* In this particular version, the children rearrange letters on a sign to read:

Please Don't Fart in a Diaper.

Laughter ensues, but it causes me to doubt the evolution of children's literature over the last 125 years.

To inspire the students to write, I play a variety of musical selections. We begin with "No Blue Thing" by Ray Lunch. I instruct the children to close their eyes, listen to the music, and then write anything that the music inspires. The responses always are delightful.

"I'm running through the tall grass through a cloud of butterflies," is a typical comment.

Then I play "Circle of Life" from the Lion King Soundtrack. Their expressions change as their imaginations play with the music. We then discuss how the music prompted images and thoughts. They are instructed to write what they envision. For the remainder of the class, I play a variety of other songs, but I always end with the same two selections. "Adagio for Strings" by Samuel Barber typically elicits strong emotions, even among the teachers. Once at Garfield Elementary, after the song a shy, little boy in the back of the room timidly raised his hand. "I see blue tears flowing down my wall," he said.

"Write about that," was my response. He seemed pleased.

The session ends with the "Hallelujah Chorus" from Handel's Messiah. Often, most of the students will sit taller and smile wider as they listen with their eyes closed. The song prompts comments such as, "I fought the dragon, and I won!"

The class can be used for early grades, too. Even if children can't yet write, they can talk. Many tell how the song helped them to remember happy or sad times. I've discovered that even though these children have less than 10 years of life, they have stories. Their responses are unfiltered and honest. My classes take an hour, and I enjoy volunteering my time with the students. It's my goal that they will use quality music (with an emphasis on quality) to inspire the muse within them. I want to challenge young people to temporarily laugh about Professor Poopypants but to wonder and write about characters as rich and provocative as Phil, the bailiff's son. No batteries required.

~

What to Wear if You Must Get Dressed

If my good jeans are in the wash and I must go out in public, choosing what to wear could challenge my most complicated decision-making abilities. Because I'm bigger than a breadbox but have the same shape, I always wear black at a public gathering because the dark color diminishes my linebacker shoulders. I'm often asked if I'm returning from a funeral.

Speaking at a writer's conference, I followed my usual procedure: Go to the podium with confidence without stumbling over a power cord. I reminded the audience to turn off cell phones and stay awake because my words could change their lives.

I learned the hard way to follow my proven dress code: I should wear dark colors, but throw in a tiny bit of color. Otherwise, I could resemble a large, woolly beast. At the Erma Bombeck conference, I obeyed my rules. I felt confident in my chosen wardrobe that included a black jacket with a turquoise shell. I was ready to mingle with other speakers and comediennes half my age, and some of us even created entire comedy routines when we met in the bathroom of the hotel.

More than 350 writers attended the conference, some with an abundant sense of style and a few who didn't care. I presented two workshops, one on publishing and one on writing humor.

For my presentations, I wore a conservative black knit dress and a long black and white tweed sweater. Ignoring my own finger puppet advice to eliminate negative self-talk, I felt like a fraud as I encouraged others to have self-confidence and revel in their majesty while I was tugging at my jacket to hide the body that longed to be a single-digit size again. But damn, the dessert cart offered cheesecake and it would go to waste if I didn't have a few samples. And it's not right to allow a bottle of wine to sit half-empty and forlorn. It must be consumed for the greater good of society.

Two weeks later at the midlife blogging conference, I mingled with more than 150 attendees. I had found my tribe. The first night, I wore a black tank top with a colorful long vest. I took a chance on going sleeveless, but no one vomited. However, for my presentation the next day, I chose a long vest again but the material was in a bulky, hairy knit of cream dappled with brown leather squares. I resembled a yak. I knew I had made a mistake as I lumbered to the podium with an Emmy award-winning screenwriter and a bestselling author. They were dressed in solid colors and both were the size of Thumbelina. I wanted to detour out the side door and join my herd of grazing animals on a hillside far, far away.

Our panel discussion was vibrant and informative, and I was grateful for the table that hid half of my body. We breezed through the presentation and no one stood to yell, "Why didn't you wear black? You always wear black!"

I continued with the outrageous fashion mistakes when I changed into a Vegas-inspired blouse for dinner. In the photos, the silly top looked like a tablecloth and I resembled a retired matron playing cards on a cruise ship. But my friends didn't seem to mind because I made them look so much better.

The event was salvaged at a Disco-themed night when I happily wiggled into my go-to black dress adorned with sparkles and bling. As the music permeated the room, I danced with wild abandon and laughed myself silly while gyrating to the beat of the Bee Gees and ABBA. The clumsy yak died and I became the Dancing Queen. It was Friday night and the lights were low. I was looking out for the place to go. I raised my arms and sang out loud.

After a few magical glasses of wine and an hour of vibrant music, I felt fantastic, dazzling, and worthy to be recognized as a bundle of shining energy. I'm sure of it, and there's no photographic evidence to prove otherwise.

Shopping for such a dress can prove daunting for any fashion-challenged woman, but for once, I'd found a fancy outfit totally out of my comfort zone. The moment I tried it on, I felt feisty, fun, and fabulously festive in my new dress festooned with fringe. The long strands covered body parts that needed to be hidden after years of neglect, gravity, and buttered scones, but the swaying material allowed gratuitous glimpses of legs that once rivaled the gams in pinup posters hung in greasy automotive shops across the country. I was one hot grandmother.

I loved my new outfit and eagerly prepared for a night at an elegant soiree. The first trial came when I attempted to pull on a coat to keep me warm against the winter chill. As I wiggled into my wrap, the fringe on the sleeves of the dress snagged, bunched, and clumped until I resembled an irritated pig wrapped in twine. Stray strands knotted around my neck and hiked the back of the dress over my butt. This was not a pretty vision, and I began to feel less glamorous.

After waddling to the car, I proceeded to the party where I encountered more challenges.

Removing the coat revealed a tangled mass of disheveled strands that seemed to be embroiled in a fight-to-the-death battle. I clawed at the material in a desperate attempt to untangle the hairball that was consuming my outfit. Once adjusted, I walked slowly so I wouldn't disrupt the delicate free flow of the garment. Static cling became the new enemy. At any given moment, a rogue fringe would leap out and adhere to the pants of a tall handsome stranger. At least my dress had good taste.

The evening progressed nicely, and I enjoyed gushing compliments about my dress. I assumed the worst was behind me and celebrated with several glasses of fine Cabernet. After a few hours, the wine needed to exit the body, so I sashayed to the restroom. This call of nature became a cry of the wild.

I proceeded to gather the fringe in a ball around my waist so I could sit and assume the position. It became apparent there wasn't any chance to control what seemed like a million independent and defiant strands, and the wine didn't help my concentration. By the time I finished my duty, I realized there was one more dilemma. One hand was needed to secure and employ the necessary toilet paper.

I shifted the wad of fringe to one side and attempted to secure it with one hand while I fumbled for the paper. The effort was futile. After achieving contortions only accomplished by professional gymnasts in the circus, I managed to drop the paper on the floor and the fringe fell into the toilet. I momentarily lost my mind.

Not one to give up easily, I grabbed more paper, finished the flush, and jumped off the comedy commode. Liquid dripped onto the floor from wet stripes of sorry, violated fringe so I grabbed sections to squeeze out the excess moisture. Soon my hands, my dress, and the entire bathroom reeked of toilet water. I washed and dried my hands, took a deep breath, and joined the party, dripping all the way, leaving a raked pattern of fringe droppings on the carpet.

I left the party and hurried home, jumped into my dowdy but fringe-free jammies, poured some hot tea, and relaxed in comfort. I may donate the dress to charity and allow someone else to enjoy its charms. But, for a brief moment in time, I felt festive and fashionable and those sweet memories will last long after the humiliation is gone. As for future fashion choices, I'll avoid the fringe element of society while I refuse to resemble a yak and aim for comfort. That makes all the decisions so much easier.

~

The Suffragist Ghosts of Susan and Alice

I had decided not to vote in the presidential election. Even though I previously had performed my loyal and patriotic duty since 1972, this year was different. The charade and parade of fools running for president made me question the need to vote. How do I select the least horrible candidate?

I believed the voting process was important to our Republic, but it was naive to think every vote counted. One candidate already had attracted large numbers of Super Delegates, those voters who were free to endorse anyone they want for nomination regardless of the voting result. Also, special-interest groups carry so much weight they can tip the scales for or against a candidate. And every election cycle brings allegations of fraud from both sides as ballots are cast multiple times, often by dead or fictitious people. What's the use?

A recent event caused me to reconsider my boycott of the elections. One evening I was working at my desk and I heard a noise in the kitchen so went to investigate. A woman sat at the table and stared at me. Too frightened to run, I stared back and mumbled, "Who are you?"

"I'm Susan Anthony," she said. "And I'm very disappointed in you."

"Would that be Susan with a 'B' Anthony?" I asked.

"Yes. You should have known by the vintage dress and white collar. Do you like my hair up in a bun like this? I could never wear it down like you do."

"It looks lovely. But how did you get in my kitchen. Aren't you dead?"

"Yes, I died in 1906. That was 14 years before women got the right to vote in this country."

I felt chagrined. I knew she was a pioneer suffragette who championed women's rights in a time when women were uneducated, couldn't own property, and had few individual rights. She proceeded to tell me about her arrest for voting in the 1872 presidential election. She wasn't allowed to speak during her trial, and the jury of all men convicted her. The judge fined her $100, which she never paid.

"I was arrested for voting," she said. "What makes you so special that you don't vote?"

I stammered an excuse and finally admitted I had no excuse.

"Would you like a glass of wine?" I asked, hoping to break the tension.

"Don't you remember I was involved in the temperance movement? I was raised a strict Quaker, and I fought against the sale of alcohol. In those days, the husband controlled everything, the finances, the house, the children, and the wife. If he got drunk every night, the wife had no power to leave. She couldn't get a divorce, and if they separated, the man usually got custody of the children and she was left destitute."

"I can't imagine how oppressive that must have been," I said. "What prompted your vocal advocacy?"

"I was a teacher and I tried to speak at the New York State Teachers' Association meeting in 1853, but the men said it wasn't proper for a woman to speak in public. They debated 30 minutes and finally relinquished. Can you imagine?"

I thought about how relatively free women are today in comparison, even though there are cloisters of fanatical societies that continue to belittle females. The fact that I could own property, have an education, travel alone, vote, run for office, and make independent decisions was due to the advocacy of brave women from the past.

Another vision appeared and a woman sat down at the table. At this point, I didn't care if Susan B. Anthony didn't drink alcohol, I poured a glass of wine. After all, it was my kitchen and I was talking with two ghosts. I welcomed the woman and asked for her story.

"I'm Alice Paul," she said. "In 1917, a group of women in Virginia was arrested, beaten, and thrown in jail for protesting for the right to vote. I was in that group and spent five weeks in prison. I went on a hunger strike so they locked me in solitary confinement in a psychiatric ward and force-fed me raw eggs through a tube down my throat. But I never gave up."

"I don't know how to repay both of you for your sacrifices," I said. "Life must have been so difficult."

"We were only two of thousands who marched in the streets, attended Congressional meetings, wrote amendments, fought with our patriarchal families, and encouraged other women. We were ridiculed, tormented, beaten, and chained to iron bars in jail cells. But we never gave up," said Paul. "Your rights today are the result of our fearless actions."

I raised my glass and toasted them. They raised empty hands to wave goodbye, smiled faintly, and began to fade away.

"I promise to vote!" I called after them.

"We know," they said in unison. "Or, we'll be back."

I decided that I would vote. Which candidate to choose remained unclear, but I would vote. Susan and Alice sacrificed too much for me to stay home in the kitchen.

~

Why Caregivers Drink

My mother terrorized several counties in southern Idaho with her erratic driving. She loved to drive fast, but often forgot about rules and regulations. Once she was speeding on the freeway and a patrol car followed her for ten miles, lights flashing, before she noticed and pulled over. She got away with just a warning because she had made some grape jelly just that morning and gave several jars to the nice officer.

I was shocked to learn that while tending my three-year-old daughter, my mother had taken her on several wild rides over country roads. My daughter was seated, unrestrained, on the console of her car as she accelerated over the hills and sailed through the air. My mother would holler "Whoop-de-doo!" and my daughter would scream with a mixture of fear and delight. After my daughter told me about the dangerous adventures with Grandma, I ended their rides together. I had grown up driving those same country roads and knew that a stalled tractor or strayed cow could easily be in the middle of the road at the bottom of the hill, waiting for a speeding grandmother to whoop-de-doo into oblivion.

Mom never wore a seat belt, despite my warnings and pleadings. She had driven for almost seven decades without a seatbelt and wasn't going to change. She was irritated when her new car made noises if the belt wasn't fastened, so she sat on the buckled belt. The least I could do was make sure her car had working airbags.

As she got older and continued to drive too fast, I received telephone calls from her worried friends. No one would drive with her, and they formed a secret society to cajole her into being a passenger in their cars. She thought she was quite special because everyone wanted to take her places. The truth was, they just wanted to get there alive.

I lived 100 miles away, but with each visit I noticed more dents and dings on her car. Soon it resembled a vehicle in a demolition derby, and I knew I had to do something. She lived alone and had been widowed for twenty-five years since my father died, and her car was her proof of independence and mobility. I was preparing The Talk about taking away the keys when another incident occurred, and this one was serious.

Mom was in her eighties when she drove her car into the back wall of her garage, panicked and threw the car into reverse and then crashed through the closing garage door behind her. The car had to go.

First, I made sure she was okay and hadn't injured her neck or back. Then I arranged for the garage wall to be fixed, a new garage door installed, and extensive damage repaired to the front and rear of her car. The car was moved to a repair shop. She remained in denial.

"There was ice on the floor and the car slipped, and I always knew the garage door was faulty," she said as I made her some tea and prepared for The Talk. "As soon as the car gets back from the shop, I'll show you I can still drive."

I poured the tea and arranged a plate of her favorite chocolate chip cookies. One bad habit I learned from my mother was to eat cookies during stressful situations. Obviously, by the increasing size of my belly, I had endured a few too many tense discussions.

"Mom, isn't it great that your friends are taking you where you need to go?" I asked, asserting my best positive attitude.

"Oh, yes," she answered. "But Evelyn drives so slowly. It took us thirty minutes to get from Wendell to Twin."

"It's a thirty-mile drive, Mom. And there are stoplights and traffic. It should take that long."

"I used to make it in 20 minutes. Even in the winter."

I cringed and silently thanked her weary guardian angels.

"Several of your friends have told me how much they enjoy your company. Couldn't we just keep that arrangement going? Maybe you don't even need a car!"

I felt my stomach churn. I didn't like parenting my mother.

She stopped mid-chew and looked at me. It was an awkward silence.

"I want my car," she said. Then she shoved the rest of the cookie into her mouth. I did the same.

An image appeared in my mind of twenty years in the future when my daughter would be attempting the same discussion with me. I grabbed another cookie. She'll have to pry those keys from my cold, dead fingers, I thought. That's when I knew The Talk was futile.

"Okay, Mom. We'll just need to wait on those darn parts to arrive."

She smiled and sipped her tea.

I didn't have the heart to tell her the repairs would take several years, and she would never drive again. Walls and doors can be repaired. A child on a bicycle was a bigger concern, and her driving wasn't safe. Every few months after the incident, she would ask about the car.

"Still in the shop waiting for parts," I would answer. She always shook her head and muttered about the lack of good customer service these days.

Mom's health began to fail, and I convinced her to move to an assisted living facility near me in Boise. The following five years brought a steady stream of calamities: a broken back, a broken hip, several falls that required stitches in her head, and several urinary tract infections. I knew the routine: the nurse would call and I would grab the Power of Attorney folder and follow the ambulance to the hospital. The admissions staff knew me by name.

"Welcome back," they would say as I rushed to the desk.

On one occasion, I provided the diagnosis. "She has a laceration to the scalp, exhibits cerebral confusion, and I recommend surgical staples," I said.

Soon I had memorized her Social Security number, supplemental health account number, allergies, prescribed medications, blood type, and history of surgeries. I could answer any question they threw at me and won an imaginary prize if she was admitted without delay. In her room, I brought ice chips, played her favorite music, and painted her toenails various colors. After receiving a sedative, she would drift off into a blessed sleep and I would find a nearby bar and order a drink. I could tell by looking around which patrons were caregivers. They were sucking back their drinks like thirsty soldiers returning from battle. We locked eyes and nodded.

The various injuries resulted in six different moves in and out of rehabilitation facilities and into different living quarters in the assisted living facilities. I packed her clothes, moved boxes, and put up her favorite photos in each new temporary place. To cheer her, I would wear a clown nose or play with finger puppets or remind her of funny stories. She would laugh sometimes and I would detect a brief sparkle in her eyes. She was entering the early stages of dementia, and on the days she remembered who I was, she would cling to my hand when I tried to leave. Several times I wept in my car.

I wasn't alone in this drama. Other caregivers shared the same emotional journey, and we passed each other in the halls as we pushed our parents in wheelchairs. Humor saved us.

"Looks like you're going places today," I said to the middle-aged woman pushing her father.

"We're thinking about the Opera!" she replied. "I must find my pearls."

"Well, Mom and I are having lunch with the Queen," I said. "They're about the same age and the Queen wants to tell Mom to have a happy birthday."

"Please bring back some scones," she said and continued down the hall.

Each day brought a new scenario. We were off to Hawaii, or planning a ride in a hot air balloon, or canning peaches for the pantry. Our parents would be lost in their own thoughts, but sometimes they rallied to join in the conversation.

"It's time for harvest," my mom said. "I'll drive to the field and watch."

The other caregiver applauded her plan and begged her to bring back photographs and stories. My mother would momentarily thrive with the memories of the harvest season and then slip back into dementia.

"Well, I hope it's a great harvest," the caretaker would say. "Bring me back some sweet corn."

I applied for and received a handicapped parking permit so I could take her to appointments. One day I needed to take her to a doctor to treat a wound that wasn't healing. I had a routine for how to get her in and out of my car. I would push her wheelchair as close as possible, open the passenger door, shove my arms underneath her arms, push the chair out of the way with my foot, and balance her against the car. Then I would place my left knee under her rump, balance her with one hand, grab onto the car, and hoist her onto the plastic-covered seat. It wasn't a pretty procedure, but it worked. I always fastened her seatbelt.

Then I would fold her chair and wedge it in the back of my car, go to the doctor, and repeat the in-and-out procedure several times. Sometimes I got a little testy and didn't play well with others, especially after waiting for an appointment for over an hour.

"The doctor is running late," a receptionist said. "Can you come back in two hours?"

I arched my aching back and then leaned closer to the woman and said, "Sure, I can return in a few hours. I'll just leave Mom here. She has a festering open wound that is attracting flies and soon she'll need help in the bathroom or she'll have an obscene accident in your waiting room. Take care of that, will you?"

It's amazing how fast the doctor's schedule cleared and we were ushered into the treatment area. The wound was treated and we were told to return in two weeks. I decided to hire a medical taxi to take us for that appointment, and kicked myself for not thinking of it sooner.

Mom became afraid of medical professionals and their needles, scissors, swabs, blood pressure machines, and temperature gauges. To encourage her, I would employ the tactics that had worked when my children were toddlers. I promised ice cream, or a trip to the zoo, or a new hat.

"They want to kill me," she said once with a serious expression. "Get me out of here."

I resorted to another strategy that had worked with my kids. I lied.

"Oh this doctor is so nice. Remember him? You taught him in Sunday School!"

My mother was proud of her days teaching youngsters at the local church. She cocked her head and then agreed. "Yes, I remember him. He'll be okay then. I wonder how his mother is doing."

After returning to her assisted living facility, she developed certain daily routines. She would wheel herself to the dinner table an hour before the meal and place napkins around her placemat as if building a protective fort around her plate. When I asked her about the action, she said other people would steal food so she had to protect it. I had seen and tasted the food. No one would want to take it.

Other times, she would greet me with stories of grand adventure. She'd tell me she had taken a walk to the grocery store and caught a bus back home. I asked her who she saw and she would say the names of all her friends and how they had a big party. Most of the people she mentioned had died years before, but I was happy they returned to see her again.

One time I took my granddaughter to visit her. Mom was overjoyed and clapped her hands. "Elaine's here!" she said. My young granddaughter seemed to understand that Mom thought she was me as a child, and my granddaughter went along with the conversation.

Mom could be convincing with her stories. Once she was highly agitated and told me her daddy was waiting outside and she had to go milk the cows. She was adamant that she couldn't be late to school. I told her the cows had been milked so it was okay. She relaxed. Several months later, she described a woman who had been sitting in her room. I asked who it was, and Mom said she didn't know but the woman was waiting for her. I took her hand, fighting with a range of emotions.

"If you're here and you're an angel," I said to the room. "Please stay with us for a while."

Mom passed away on the first day of November, and family and friends came from miles around to celebrate her life. I returned to her room a week after the funeral to collect and move her things for the last time. I had to hurry because the room was being prepared for another resident. I left a clown nose on the closet shelf.

~

How to Plan a Funeral

After my mother's death, I switched roles from caregiver to being the designated funeral planner. I arranged an appointment with the funeral director and silently entered the stately building, stepping alone into a world that revolved around the business of death. For added strength, I carried the one thing I knew would please my mother: a jar of her homemade grape jelly.

The interior smelled of old roses and candles. Boxes of tissue perched at regular intervals on the cupboards as I walked down the hallway. Pleasant artwork featuring gentle landscapes, sunsets, and flowers covered the walls and hung over stuffed, worn couches. Soft music played from invisible speakers. It seemed to be an ancient parlor for afternoon tea or a lady's luncheon, except there was an open casket on display in the viewing room. I lingered before tiptoeing into the room. I could see the body of an older man, his hands resting across his chest, his mouth unusually tight, his glasses oddly out of place.

"May I help you?"

"Shit!" I exclaimed as a voice caused me to jump.

I turned to see the funeral director coming into the room.

"I'm sorry, but you scared me," I said. I noticed his nametag, Leroy Brown, Funeral Director. My nervous energy wanted to sing the Jim Croce song, "Bad, bad Leroy Brown. Baddest man in the whole damn town." But, I recovered my composure.

"Don't worry," Leroy Brown said. "Let's go to my office. Mr. Marshall here is expecting visitors soon."

I turned and paid my respects to the corpse of Mr. Marshall and followed Mr. Brown to his office, wondering if he was meaner than a junkyard dog.

His office was a miniature version of the front parlor: bland but sensible furniture, a simple desk, landscape portraits, and more boxes of tissues. I could really add some color to this room, I thought. He was dressed in a conservative suit without a tie, and his hair was parted in the middle and resembled the styles I'd seen in old black-and-white photos. His hands were white and smooth, definitely not those of a farmer or mechanic, and I remembered that part of his job was to handle dead bodies.

I set the jar of jelly on his desk. He looked puzzled.

"It's from Mom," I said. "She'd want you to have it."

He smiled faintly and we settled into our chairs. He cleared his throat and began to speak softly with compassion. I wondered how many times he had given the same talk.

"I'm sorry about your loss," he said. "I'm sure she was a good woman."

I bit my tongue to keep from yelling, "Good woman! Mister, she was a Saint! She put up with me and a ton of crap for years. Women less than that got pyramids and the Taj Mahal." But I nodded and retrieved my notebook.

We reviewed the date and place for the funeral. I would be responsible for arranging speakers, music, and the reception. The meeting was fine until he asked a simple question.

"What do you want her to wear?"

As much as I had anticipated the question, it still carried an important decision about her final outfit. I knew she would prefer her colorful appliquéd sweatshirt, black knit pants, and sturdy oxfords. She had a collection of tops adorned with flowers, birds, and holiday scenes that she ordered from her favorite *Country Living* catalog. They were comfortable and washable, her pragmatic requirement for anything she wore. For my daughter's wedding, I had to gently suggest she change from her favorite purple sweatshirt with glittery hummingbirds to a more appropriate black one. She reluctantly agreed.

But for her funeral, I had a different idea, and she couldn't stop me.

"The nice robe," I answered. "With the pearl necklace."

The man stopped writing and peered at me, unsure of what I had suggested.

"You want her buried in a robe?"

I explained that in 1969, my father had traveled to Japan on a business trip and brought home an elegant silk robe as a gift for my mother. They had been high school sweethearts. He was the gregarious student body president and she was the timid valedictorian. They began life together with nothing but ambition and built a successful business. But he was never one for giving gifts and she wasn't comfortable accepting them.

Over the past 45 years, I'd asked her why she never wore the robe, and her answer always was the same: "It's too nice."

That's how she lived, protecting special objects in her life that she never felt worthy enough to enjoy. She never burned the fancy candles so they melted in storage. The good china dishes and silverware only came out at Thanksgiving and Christmas. And, she saved and reread every birthday and holiday card she ever received. (I inherited this trait, and it was a tough one to break.)

To arrange for her service, my to-do list was filled with complicated assignments. How did I get the headstone engraved? It had been waiting at my father's grave since 1989. How did I condense her amazing life into a 300-word obituary? Should I request that in lieu of flowers, people contribute to the scholarship she established at the University of Idaho? The donation would be nice, but she also would have loved the flowers. She'd say she didn't deserve them and they were too nice, but she would have loved the flowers. The only *easy* decision to make was what she would wear for her final outfit. While her health deteriorated and Hospice was called to assist, I'd had the robe professionally cleaned and ready.

She wore the nice robe for the first time at her funeral service. And she wore her pearls. She always wore pearls, even with her favorite cozy sweatshirts. She was beautiful.

I've helped organize weddings, including a few of my own, but planning a funeral is a different type of hectic and emotional activity with a demanding timeline. The details could leave you breathless. Oops, wrong word.

In a wedding, you have months to prepare. With a funeral, you have days and you'll need to interrupt your own grieving to organize the details. A few generations ago, the family would clean and dress the body, prop it on the dining table next to the potato salad, throw a party, and then bury the dearly departed in the family plot on a nearby hill. Now, there is a complicated checklist that rivals the NASA instructions for a lunar landing to make sure your loved one has a proper burial.

Because everyone eventually dies, someday you may need to organize a funeral. Here are some helpful tips.

1. Don't lose the body. As previously mentioned, my mother's body was temporarily lost. I don't advise the conundrum when one is attempting to plan a funeral.

2. Don't allow details to be the death of you. Notify key family members, but tell them you don't need any help because planning through a committee could be fatal. Open a sack of cookies, sit down with a notebook or computer, and begin to make decisions: choose pall bearers, write the obituary, approve the death certificate, notarize details for the IRS, finalize the funeral place and program, choose the music and soloists, arrange for food and flowers, contact the cemetery, make decisions about embalming and donations, and decide what clothes the person will wear. Some families request a certain hairdresser, but the funeral home can make those arrangements. Do you want rings removed? Do you want the casket with the pretty roses or the sunset? And, don't forget to make a memorial video to be shown at the funeral. Do all this in a few days while keeping a stiff upper lip. Sorry, wrong word again.

3. Don't present a stupid program. If you think Aunt Bernice will go to the podium and wail for 20 minutes, discreetly suggest she save her remarks for the reception,

preferably after the first two rounds of drinks. If you want to include some literary orations, avoid Robert Service's famous poem, "The Cremation of Sam McGee." And, finally, if all your music sounds like the "The Funeral March of the Marionette" followed by a requiem, a dirge, and a lone bagpiper, expect some of your guests to fall onto the ground and beg to be the next to die.

4. Don't overwhelm the undertaker. I'm thankful I chose a reputable funeral director instead of Billy Bob's Burial and Tire Changing Service. After my mother died, I had numerous questions. The funeral director patiently listened when I called in alarm and asked who would dig the grave. "We'll handle everything, ma'am," he said. I was so relieved that I wouldn't need to ask my son to bring a shovel and a backhoe.

5. Don't turn the funeral into a bazaar. I once attended a wedding where one of the guests brought along Cutco knives to sell to the attendees. This is not appropriate for weddings or funerals. Even though I'll have a captive, emotional audience, I didn't plan on arranging a book signing event after my mother's service. She always bragged to her friends that I wrote books, even though she never read any of them. I told her I wrote under the pen name of J.K. Rowling.

6. Don't allow expenses to haunt you. You may need to dig deep to unearth some money because the base cost for a funeral can range from $5,000 to $10,000. The choices vary from a pine box tossed into a swamp to an elaborate $25,000 casket carried by a procession of white limousines into a private plot. If you're hosting a boisterous

reception after the funeral, save enough money to buy some quality liquor because you care enough to say goodbye with a fine Scotch instead of cheap moonshine.

7. Don't forget the living. After the funeral is over, use your energy and emotions to appreciate and connect with those around you. There are still a lot of people who aren't dead yet, and some of them need a friend.

8. Don't stop celebrating life. If anyone cares to organize a funeral for me (after I'm dead, of course), I want a full marching band to play John Philip Sousa marches and an open bar with plenty of exquisite Cabernet. And, I'm requesting lots of pie with ice cream because gaining weight will *finally* no longer be an issue.

~

Happy Hour, At Last!

Sue, my fashionable friend, called with great news.

"Get out of your yoga pants. There's a sale on ankle pants and we're going shopping!"

"Why can't you ever find a sale on Cakebread Cabernet?" I asked, acknowledging my failure in the fashion arena. "And what's wrong with my pants?"

"You haven't updated your wardrobe since the Bush administration. The last item of clothing you purchased was a pair of wool socks that had pictures of elk."

"I love my socks."

"Well, you can't wear socks with ankle pants, so change your outfit and let's go."

My closet resembled a boxcar full of mismatched heaps of donated clothing bound for a foreign country. Single shoes mingled with belts and purses while tailored suits fought for space among the t-shirts, golf clothes, and jeans in three sizes. I had a difficult time parting with anything, especially my small jeans that I once actually zipped. Now they wouldn't go over my knee, but I keep them just in case I magically drop fifty pounds. It could happen!

I occasionally glance at fancy magazines that show photos of closets organized by people who don't share my sense of creative chaos. We would never be close friends. Their shoes are packed in separate plastic boxes and displayed by season and color. Their dresses hang on padded hangers and sweaters are neatly folded, separated by color-coordinated tissue paper. Pants are strategically stacked on space-saving hangers and a few empty, dusted shelves display ornamental candles and plaques with sentimental sayings. Who does that shit?

My long skirts and dresses are smashed together with a silk kimono I found in Hong Kong ten years ago but hadn't worn, a ragged assortment of moisture-wicking, menopause nightgowns, and three long leather jackets I bought in various sizes but are too hot to wear (because of the menopause). A drunken party of purses that range in value from free-with-a-purchase to costs-more-than-a-vacation fill tubs on the floor beside baskets bulging with unused age-defying lotions because I haven't defied it yet. A favorite sweatshirt from college joins the colorful collection of dusty workout clothes, floral Hawaiian prints that I can't wear in public, and a beautiful silk blouse I wore once. A fastidious person would enter my closet and immediately suffer from sudden cardiac arrest, and I would feel guilty so I never invite just anyone to see it.

I recently bought new carpet for the master bedroom and panicked when I realized the installers would also do the closet. Moving a king-sized bed and two heavy dressers was much easier than finding the floor of my closet. After I cleared off the clutter and dumped it in the bathtub, I was surprised that the floor already *was* covered in carpet. Who knew?

A current bestselling book about organization says to hold each item and only keep the ones that bring joy. It would take me years to touch and analyze each item and decide its joyful value. A silk kimono from Hong Kong! That was valuable.

I own approximately 25 cardigan sweaters in a variety of colors, like black, off-black, dark gray, true-black, and charcoal. I pair them with black pants and a colored shell. It's my go-to, middle-age, pleasantly plump uniform. The dark outfit helps hide back fat rolls if someone snaps a photograph of my backside and posts it on social media. People who do that usually spend hours to touch up and alter their own images but take nasty delight in publishing ghastly photos that make others appear to be auditioning for "The Walking Dead." These foul photo friends deserve to be purged from all contact lists.

After Sue called, I stood in my closet and tried to decide what to wear. After trying on several outfits that brought me varying degrees of joy, I settled on black pants, a colorful shell, and a black sweater. I finished the ensemble with black socks and black leather ankle boots. Even though I could double as a retired biker of dubious character and suspicious pedigree, the outfit remains my uniform of choice. Sue arrived at the door, resplendent in fitted, white cropped pants, a cream and gold blouse, and a flowing scarf that reminded me of a World War II flying ace but without the airplane. Her shoes were so pointed I wondered if she had cut off a few toes.

"I hate you," I said as I opened the door and observed her impeccable style.

"Oh my," she replied. "You're wearing black pants and a black sweater. Have you changed your outfit since last year?"

"The last person who told me what to wear was my mother when I was in elementary school. I didn't listen then so why should I care what you say?"

Sue shook her head, marched into my closet, screamed out loud, and after rummaging for a few minutes returned with a red blouse and matching sweater, some cropped tan pants, and my best tan sandals. She muttered about needing surgical gloves and antiseptic spray.

"Here," she said. "Wear these and we'll roll up your pants. We're looking for ankle pants, so the socks and boots must go, too, and lose the baggy sweater so you don't resemble a waif from the cast of *Les Miserables*."

"Resemble a waif?" I laughed. "Aren't waifs skinny? I look more like Madame Thénardier, the innkeeper's plump wife in the musical."

"Yes," she mused. "I do see the similarities."

To humor her, I changed my clothes and we drove to a lovely boutique selling ankle pants. I asked Sue what was so special about the pants and why they were priced more than long pants that had more material.

"Ankle pants are the latest fashion statement for women over fifty," she replied. "We only need to expose our delicate ankles and leave the rest to imagination."

"I can imagine my leg. It doesn't bring me joy but I can't discard it."

Sue parked the car and we entered the store. Two sales associates name Buffy and Miranda floated over to us with a gracious welcome appropriate for dignitaries. Buffy focused on Sue and led her away to the front of the store with festive racks that featured the latest arrivals.

Miranda looked at me as a butcher would study a freshly killed steer.

"What can we do here?" she muttered to herself. She ushered me to the sales rack and pulled out several pairs of ankle pants and a few tops. I disappeared into a changing room and pulled out my phone to check e-mail messages.

"How's it going in there?" Miranda chirped after a few minutes.

"Just fine."

I dropped the phone into my purse, pulled off my clothes, and wiggled into a pair of white pants and a flowing, oversized green blouse. I walked barefoot to the big mirror and contemplated the image. I looked like a big olive plopped onto two toothpicks. Immediately, I craved a martini.

"You look fun!" Miranda exclaimed as if I were the model for all older women who wanted to be regarded as fun.

"I think I look like a fat olive."

"Don't be silly. See how the ankle pants highlight your perfect ankles?"

I looked down and noticed the unsightly spider veins choking my ankles, the wilted skin covered with age spots, and the scruffy heels that were rough enough to rip leather upholstery.

"You should sell used cars," I said. "These pants look like I've had a growth spurt."

"Don't be silly," she said, again. "The tapered legs meet exactly at your ankle. That's why they're called ankle pants!"

I had no reply for that astute observation except to note that a robot wouldn't have been so patronizing. I had always advocated the use of automated, computerized sales clerks in all dressing rooms for women over fifty. That would eliminate so much annoying small talk.

Sue emerged from a dressing room and pranced in front of the mirror in her black cropped pants, colored tank top, and tight black sweater. It was similar to my outfit she had mocked at my house.

"Have you changed your outfit since last year?" I asked.

She laughed and posed for her reflection.

"This is a modern but classic style," she said. "And it doesn't require socks."

"That's too bad. A pair of elk socks would look fabulous with those pants."

She bought the entire set and I only purchased the pants because I wanted to practice highlighting my perfect ankles. We walked out of the store and Sue pulled me into the next shop featuring jewelry in various stages of bling and price.

"Women over fifty don't wear as much bling anymore," the saleswoman said as she displayed a simple pendant on a silver chain. "And this captivating style draws the eyes away from a loose neck or double chin."

I fingered my Swarovski crystal earrings, multiple chains with a medallion covered with bling, and bracelet heavy with rhinestone charms. I had estimated that an abundance of bling would detract from all the skin lollygagging around my neck.

"I do bling," I said. "My favorite dress is covered with rhinestones and studs. When I wear it, I become the Dancing Queen."

"That's a great attitude," the saleswoman said, not wanting to lose a sale. "You should have and wear as much bling as you want."

I purchased some dangly earrings that were sparkly enough to show through my long hair. Sue bought the pendant, confident it would highlight her enhanced bosom and diminish her middle-aged chin.

"Isn't this fun?" she squealed, shuffling her shopping bags.

"Sure," I answered. "Let's eat."

We found an outside table at a charming restaurant and ordered salads and ice tea, the go-to late lunch for women over fifty. I only ordered a salad as a noble experiment and because Sue suggested we try to lower our intake of carbohydrates. I was beginning to question our friendship. I normally ordered pasta and cheesecake and washed it down with a delicate Pinot Noir.

People scurried past on various missions, and I noticed the usual characters in the unplanned parade of my life. Young lovers sauntered by, and I smiled even as they ignored me. Their clothes were carefree and their behavior was positive. They possessed that momentary magic of young love, before the serious realities of life and responsibilities fractured their focus. I vaguely remembered those days of hot passion, cool attitudes, multiple choices, and few worries.

Harried mothers pushed strollers bigger than my first car. Their hair was clamped in lopsided ponytails, and their clothes revealed puke on their shoulders, peanut butter on their pants, and bulging seams in tight blouses. They randomly threw goldfish crackers to cranky toddlers who blew snot bubbles and cried for candy. I wanted to tell them their kids grow up in about two days. Soon they'll have time and energy to wear nice clothes, speak in complete sentences, go to the bathroom alone, enjoy sex without locking the bedroom door, and carry purses without wet wipes.

Executive women in their thirties walked briskly, cell phones to their ears, discussing strategies and appointments. Their suits were tailored, their hair shaped in perfect bobs, and they carried leather briefcases as billboards of success. I wanted to tell them to slow down, because I knew where they had been and where they were going. The memory made me tired.

Older people shuffled slower. Many wore their best clothes with a prominence of tweed, lace, and floral patterns from another era. They were beyond caring about the latest fashion and were content to be living. I imagined their closets contained hat boxes and little silk pillows full of scented potpourri. I smiled at the older couples who looked and dressed alike and watched as the single ones ambled along.

Sue interrupted my thoughts. "I wonder if I need a new jacket," she said.

"I've read that women over fifty only need twelve items: a jacket, a cardigan sweater, two pairs of pants, two skirts, four tops, and two dresses," I said. "Who can do that? I could dress two dozen women with the clothes in my closet."

"About your closet..."

"Stop. I promise to get to it. It's a delicate process."

"Do you want me to help?"

"No! You might throw out my suits with the padded shoulders. They might come back in style."

"They're twenty years old! And padded shoulders made you look like a bison."

I paused to analyze her comment. "A bison? I looked like a buffalo?"

I made a mental note to remove all the clothes that had been hanging in the closet for more than five years. That represented more than half of what I owned, and I knew it would be a difficult task. I briefly considered adding a closet in the garage, but that wouldn't solve the problem. I decided that I didn't need my corporate business suits anymore. My life had evolved, for the better.

Sue seemed to sense my pensive mood. "Oh look," she said. "It's time for Happy Hour."

I perked up and motioned for the waitress. She came over smiling and asked if we wanted any drinks.

"You know us so well," I said and requested two glasses of red wine.

I thanked her for her positive attitude and asked how long she had worked at the restaurant.

"I've been here two years, and I'm working my way through college," she said. "I only have one more year until graduation."

"That's wonderful," said Sue. "You have the best outlook on life, and I'm sure you'll find success."

"Thanks," she said. "Someday I hope to earn some time to relax with friends, just like you're doing."

"That time will come before you know it," I said. "Then you can start your own Midlife Happy Hour Club."

She turned to fetch our drinks. When she returned, we held our wine glasses and toasted to her and to our successful mission of finding just the right pair of ankle pants.

"I shall wear them soon to show off my perfect ankles," I said. "I'll save the elk socks for winter."

I looked up to notice more people coming and going in various directions as their workday was ending. Some were rushing, others lingering, and a few looked at us and smiled.

"Look at all these people passing by," I said. "They're all in various stages of life. Right now, I think midlife is the best time to be alive. It's like Happy Hours. We've finished the hard work, and now we can relax and enjoy ourselves. And we're sure as hell not ready yet for closing time."

We finished our drinks and ordered another round. After all, it was Happy Hour.

~

Acknowledgments

Thanks to AK Turner for abundant encouragement and astute editing, even though she's decades away from *Midlife Happy Hour*.

Thanks to Sarah Tregay for cover and layout design—and nonjudgmental patience.

Thanks to my real midlife friends, Linda, Nancy, Jennifer, Debby, Kitty, and Mary, and to my pretend friend, Sue, who somehow made it into the book.

Thanks to my granddaughters, Luciya, Mirabel, Brooke, Zoe, Eva, and Eryn, who make me laugh and feel young again.

And thanks to handsome Ken (Studley), who inspired the clever cover design using an hourglass and wine glass while we were sitting on the deck at the cabin sipping adult beverages. The party continues.